David Ress

Market Manipulation and The Price of Eggs

A Microhistory of Free Markets and Artificial Prices

David Ress
School of Humanities
University of New England
Richmond, VA, USA

ISBN 978-3-031-87170-2   ISBN 978-3-031-87171-9 (eBook)
https://doi.org/10.1007/978-3-031-87171-9

Cover credit: © Melisa Hasan

This Palgrave Macmillan imprint is published by the registered company Springer Nature Switzerland AG
The registered company address is: Gewerbestrasse 11, 6330 Cham, Switzerland

If disposing of this product, please recycle the paper.

Market Manipulation and The Price of Eggs

For Karen, Morgan and Jared

PREFACE

I had thought, reporting on the Eurobond market for Reuters, that I understood financial markets, though the boom in a bit of financial legerdemain, perpetual floating rate notes ("perps")—debt in which the principal was never repaid—and the innovation of New Zealand dollar denominated paper paying twice the interest rate of the more usual Euro-dollar, or offshore sterling, Swiss franc, Deutschemark or yen paper baffled me. Why would the World Bank, say, want to borrow New Zealand dollars and pay interest on them at fourteen or fifteen percent, when what the bank was funding with that borrowing were its loans, in U.S. dollars, and at much lower rates to developing countries? The clue here came when my friend Bernie Gadow, who led the syndication desk at a big Japanese bank (it went bust a dozen years later), patiently explained that there was a whole other market going on, a market in a complex web of swaps: a market, that is, in derivative instruments. These swaps might include a New Zealand bank's contracted exchange of its foreign currency holdings for, in this case, the World Bank's proceeds from its "Euro-kiwi" bond. There would be, as well, an interest rate the New Zealand bank paid on those New Zealand dollars, a rather lower rate than it would pay on domestic deposits or the wholesale money market because tax authorities cannot lay hands on income from Eurobonds—a market that exists as a tax free zone. In exchange, the New Zealander bank might require a more advantageous rate on the foreign currency it swapped. The rates of interest, the gaps between them, the currency exchange ratio and the calculations and recalculations over the course of the two- to five-year life of the bond of those rates that would determine the amounts of who paid what to whom were what this derivative market traded. Euro-kiwis, meanwhile, were aimed at an atypical buyer—they sold in tiny denominations, just $1,000, essentially aimed at individuals (not banks or institutional investors) outside New Zealand (New Zealanders would be taxed when repatriating income from the bonds). These were speculators who likely missed the message inherent in a fourteen or fifteen percent interest rate: that there was a general perception of a rather large risk that the value of the currency would decline, thanks to New Zealand's then-high inflation rate and what was at the time still a somewhat shaky economy.

Newly arrived in London after covering banks and public finance in Montreal and not understanding how perps could have any value for their bank purchaser—and uncertainty that would soon be expressed by bank regulators—I got my clue here from the senior trader at a French bank, whose job was to sell new floating rate note issues to clients. Slumped in a chair at the trading desks, Alec bemoaned his bank's decision to take a chunk of a new perp, complaining it was a real dog, before the phone rang and a syndicate manager from a smaller bank that had been left out of the floater's underwriting group, and who evidently thought it a better deal than Alec did, asked about buying some. They dickered for a bit, struck a price: "Yours!" Alec shouted, slamming down the phone, the sale done. "Yours! Large amounts!" he repeated, grinning broadly. He had, he explained, dumped the dog on a sucker—and at a mark-up over what his bank had paid.

A lot of the $20 plus billion worth of perps issued in the mid-1980s traded that way: it was a market pretty much between banks, many of whom issued them, bought other banks' and happily quoted two-way prices—ready to buy or sell at any moment to any of the other several dozen players in the market. Typically traded in lots of $5 million, this was wholesale funding for any bank issuing the paper; rates were pegged a bit above the London Interbank Offered Rate for short-term loans between banks; the usual rate on a perp was pegged at 10 to 15 basis points above to three-month LIBOR. The only way this made sense on such nominally long-term—infinite term, really—paper was the assurance that a holder could also sell the note. Until, all of sudden, in December 1986, nobody could. In a sense the trading in perps and their related swaps were markets on markets—not only on one another but also on much wider market for bank loans, a market that touches the daily lives of people far from those London trading rooms.

My bafflement about perps, my bemusement with Euro-kiwis has never really gone away, and it informs the tale about markets I would like to tell here: a tale about different markets on markets, of trading in derivative instruments. So this is a microhistory of a deal in fresh egg futures contracts—a history that lets us ask, as any wiseacre might of any rambling, random tale: what's that got to do with the price of eggs? As I hope readers will when I tell this tale, Sushil Wadhwani, then with the London School of Economics, and Sykes Welford, now with The Citadel, both put up with my fumbling efforts as a reporter covering Eurobond markets to relate what I thought I saw in financial markets with the economic theory I thought I understood. The late Tom Askimakopolus of McGill University introduced me to an approach to theory and analysis that underly my little history of some derivatives trades and the artificial prices that resulted, as have my continued explorations with Carl Colonna of Christopher Newport University into Keynesian, post-Keynesian and Austrian theory. Jennifer Clark, of the University of Adelaide, and David Roberts, of the University of New England (Australia), have over the years tried to keep my ventures in the history of popular ideas of economics and law in focus, as have the social history and historiography I studied with Matthew Dillon and Richard Scully at UNE. Any errors that follow, of course, are entirely my own.

Richmond, VA, USA   David Ress

CONTENTS

About the Author

David Ress is a research associate of the University of New England (Australia) and the author of Municipal Accountability in the America Age of Reform (2017); Deeds, Titles and Changing Concepts of Land Rights (2020); and The Kansas Blue Sky Act (2023).

CHAPTER 1

What's That Got to Do with the Price of Eggs?

Abstract A minute of drama on the floor of the Chicago Mercantile Exchange on June 25, 1968 moved the price of futures in fresh eggs to a level that regulators would later say was artificially high. Their finding marked the first time they penalized a trader for a market manipulation that did not involve a market corner or squeeze or outright fraud. Their analysis would be definitively overturned a half century later, but it posed a fundamental question about financial markets: could they generate artificial prices or do the dynamics of a free market with informed actors inevitably determine the real value of goods and services.

Keywords Futures markets · Derivative securities · Market manipulation · Price theory · Artificial price

With a minute to go before trading in Chicago Mercantile Exchange futures contracts for fresh (shell) eggs was to end for the day on June 25, 1968, floor brokers' desultory attention was on the blackboard where an exchange employee had chalked up the eight still open offers for November delivery of fresh eggs. Egg futures were not moving much that day. The last completed trade had happened more than 40 minutes earlier at 40.3 cents per dozen, for a standard car-lot of 600 cases of 30 dozen eggs. That 40.3 cent deal was the day's high, and as if uncertain where to go next—for the remaining eight open offers to sell ranged at prices between 40.2 and 41.30 cents—the brokers had done nothing for that 40 minute-plus span of time. Then, as most were thinking that they were done for the day, David Henner, a 20-year veteran of the Mercantile Exchange trading floor, called out: "I'll buy the board"; that is, that he would buy all eight offers. Seconds later and even more dramatically, with the bell to close the day's session about to sound, he called out a bid for one more contract, at 41.85 cents, the maximum price allowed for the day by a Mercantile Exchange rule aimed at reining in some of the games-playing for which the egg futures market had become notorious. For several seconds, nobody knew what to do; a dozen traders quickly gathered around.[1]

Let's pause here, with that huddle of confused floor brokers as they tried to figure out what was happening—and as we try, too. For the egg futures ring at that moment was one of those places where it was not clear what the price of something really was, to say nothing of what the price really ought to be, which is not necessarily the same thing. What is about to happen in the next few seconds is a window into the mechanics of markets, in this case, a market that appears close to the ideal market of theory: buyer versus seller, buyer versus buyer, seller versus seller, all of them in a vigorous competition. Here, it is the interaction of buyers and sellers—in this case, Henner and the other floor brokers—that fixes the true value of goods and services. What is about to happen in the shell egg futures pit did not, a federal regulator will eventually say. A half century later, however, a federal appeals court judge would rule that a not-dissimilar pattern of bids in a different market did generate a real price. The microscopic history of these moments of buying and selling can be, I suggest, a macroscopic history of ideas about prices and markets and the value of things.

The trade Henner is about to conclude will lead to a legal finding that he created a false price and had therefore manipulated a market. The other traders on the floor that day might have simply said Henner had been tricky or had played unfairly, but a federal regulator's finding that Henner had broken the law marked a return to a long forgotten question that had troubled the first political economists: when is the price at which goods are bought and sold not the real value of those goods. The Henner decision, the first time a finding of market manipulation did not involve a fraud or a market corner put the issue squarely. Henner did not control enough supply or represent enough demand to move prices when he called out his bid. Instead, he had merely staged a bit of theatre. That drama was enough to move the price of the November 1968 shell egg future, and Department of Agriculture Judicial Officer Donald Campbell would call that a false price and market manipulation. A half century later, prices from the same kind of end-of-session drama would instead seem to confirm a free market's purpose to federal appeals court judge Richard Sullivan. The market in this view, that is, was always right.

Sullivan's view of markets is one that had gained much ground through the 1960s, a time when more and more Americans directed their savings to financial markets. Small speculators' activity in shell egg futures roughly quadrupled in 1968, for instance. The view of markets that informed Sullivan's decision sees them as impersonal, rather like a machine, where, as the economist Milton Friedman wrote: "All take prices as given by the market and no individual can by himself have more than a negligible influence on price."[2] Yet when David Henner bid 41.85 cents, he set the closing price for the future, one that was as high as possible.

It was a price that, in theory, could lead farmers to decide how many eggs to deliver and wholesalers to decide what they would pay for eggs. For speculators who believed in the astrology of plotting price patterns on charts, it was supposedly a price that could signal whether to buy futures or not. That the impact of a shell egg futures contract closing price might not have had either impact is not really the point here: I am interested in why so many, including Judicial Officer Campbell and Judge Sullivan, thought it did, and why the one thought a trade could yield an artificial price when the other did not.

For Campbell, if Henner's inexplicably sharply higher bid at the closing bell were to be accepted as a real, valid price, "No one would know whether a particular futures price reflected the best judgment of traders … based on their expectations of future supply and demand conditions," and if no one could know that "Futures trading, as we know it today, would go out of existence. It would serve no useful purpose"—price discovery, in this case, of eggs.[3] Reflecting on the hundreds of millions of dollars traders lost because of DRW Investments' carefully timed bids for interest rate derivatives, Judge Sullivan concluded that "It is not illegal to be smarter than your counterparties."[4] In a sense, he concluded, markets were about winning and losing,

The price discovery that Campbell believed was the primary function of a futures market is not the same thing as confirming a price by buying something and going home with it. The separation of the price discovery function from price-setting is fundamental to any derivative instrument, whether a futures contract, an option or a swap. Each is a financial contract for the supposed exchange of an underlying asset, a contract that can be bought and sold separately from that asset. It is easy to create a derivative—easier, for instance, to call out "I'll buy the board" or "41.85" than to trudge out to a hen house every morning to make sure the chickens are fed and the eggs are collected—and easy, if not necessary painless, to take a profit or accept a loss. All that is required is to buy or sell a mirror image instrument. A derivative is a proxy for the underlying asset, but its price is subject to what any two traders are willing to offer and bid for reasons that have nothing to do with the effort of creating or acquiring the underlying asset. Traders here trade perceptions, not products, and it is this trade in perception that is what supposedly endows futures markets with their price discovery function.

Derivatives, then, bind prices in a single current instant to perceptions about the future: the "jam to-morrow and jam yesterday – but never jam to-day," that the White Queen offered Alice in Wonderland. If the ease of putting a price on future events—the price of eggs or the spread between short- and long-term interest rates—might seem to inspire caution and analysis, it can also fuels the bold buys or large shorts that generate wild price swings.[5] David Henner did not, as it happens, move egg prices in grocery stores—but as one landmark court case on artificial prices noted, one speculator's big purchases of July 1931 Chicago Board of Trade corn future prompted so many shipments of grain to Chicago that Iowa farmers could not find enough feed for their hogs and cattle while some $6.4 billion-worth of simultaneous purchase and sale of matching electricity supply derivatives drove the wholesale price of electricity in California up from $30 a megawatt to about $300 in 2000; the decisions power plants made about when to fire up or shut down generators in response so threatened the state's somewhat fragile electric grid that the system's managers had to impose rolling blackouts.[6] When the average price of a gallon of regular unleaded gasoline jumped from $1.46 per gallon in 2000 to $3.14 per gallon in September 2005 and the price of natural gas—the most important home-heating fuel and a critical source of power and feedstock for industry—rose from $2 per million British Thermal Units to as much as $8, leading the U.S. Senate Permanent Subcommittee on Investigations concluded that when speculators "have been pouring billions of dollars" into futures, options and swaps, they "have, in effect, created an additional demand for oil, driving up the price."[7] Almost from the start of trading in futures, producers and consumers of foodstuffs have pressured government to regulate these markets; this is why market regulators have been so concerned about artificial prices, for all that those regulators have struggled, without success, to say what price manipulation is.[8]

Price discovery, that intermediation of the current moment with a potential future that is the essential purpose of derivatives trading, is also a primary function of secondary markets in stocks and bonds. What people are willing to pay for existing securities—that is, stocks and bonds that have already performed their function of raising investment funds for enterprises—supposedly signals to businesses the likely cost of new capital. And just as Judicial Officer Campbell was moved to ask if Henner's June 25 mini-drama distorted a price, it is possible to ask if the much larger drama of, for example, the final days of October 1929 on Wall Street is also a story of distorted prices. So, on Black Thursday, tinplate manufacturer Follansbee Brothers might report a 50% increase in dividends it would be paying and still see its shares fall from $64.87-1/2 to $52, in the hours that followed, a twenty percent decline.[9]

"Prices are a market phenomenon" that "cannot be constructed synthetically" as the economist Ludwig von Mises (along with so many others) tells us. It is vain to think there might be a better way, von Mises writes, and "It is no less vain to ponder on what prices ought to be."[10] Yet people do ponder exactly that. Futures brokers and Judicial Officer Campbell will in the next chapter explain why Henner's 41.85 cents seemed unreal and out of step with market consensus; the chapter after that will detail the reasons for Campbell's concerns: price signaling, particularly for the small, inexpert and distant speculators who decided to buy or sell based on reported closing price trends as well as a major legal rebuff recent case involving a cotton futures market manipulation.

Henner here, by offering to sell a contract to buy eggs in November, was trading much as did the bartering farmers and vintners who early theorists of market mechanics used to explain how markets work, as we will see in Chapter 4. A discussion of some of the harder-to-model energy involved when trading in competitive markets and the challenges of understanding traders' intentions are the subject of the next two chapters, which set the stage for a chapter discussing Henner's subsequent trading in pork belly futures and the problem defining market manipulation. Here, James M. Stone. a former chairman of the Commodity Futures Trading Commission, will explain here is that saying when a price is artificial is hard to do "since neither supply schedules nor demand schedules have tangible manifestations."[11] In conclusion, a look at the DRW case of 2018, which like Henner's trading, also involved carefully timed bidding to move a derivative price will suggest the question of whether a price is artificial or not is ultimately a matter of faith—a faith in free, competitive markets that can be at times misplaced.

On the avowedly free market of the Chicago Mercantile Exchange floor, Henner was competing, though the initial confusion in the egg futures pit and the complaints that followed suggested this was far from ordinary market competition. Henner thought, too, that he saw something in the market to justify that 41.85 cent bid—though what and in which market was not obvious to anyone else. Henner would suggest that what he saw the price needed to secure one last November futures contract before the closing bell, as he positioned himself for a rise in the price of real eggs later in the year. Campbell believed that what Henner saw was the way his bid would affect the pattern of prices of egg futures on a chart. In any event, Henner jumped—and, as it turned out, jumped the wrong way, whether he was reacting to the production of eggs or the pattern of prices, whether cool, calculating manipulation or something more like a reflex. Perhaps, then, the tale of the shell egg futures pit points us in a direction that the economist John Maynard Keynes, a successful speculator in futures himself, suggested when he wrote about the "animal spirits" and preference for action than for inaction that drive so many decisions about what to do with our money.[12]

Or, perhaps, the question then is rather like the old catch phrase from American comic writing: the one that, for instance, Roberts DeSaussure Newhall posed to his fictional newsboy Jimmy after Jimmy called his attention to an advertisement for a used tuxedo. "Well," Newhall says "What's that got to do with the price of eggs?" and got a long, sad story about Jimmy's dating disappointments.[13] And so, we'll ask, as Henner calls our attention to the November future: What's that got to do with the price of eggs?

NOTES

1. In re David G Henner, 30 Agricultural Decisions 1151, at 1162.
2. Milton Friedman, *Capitalism and Freedom* (Chicago: University of Chicago Press, 1982 [first published 1962]), 102.
3. In re Henner, at 1241.

4. Memorandum and Opinion, Commodity Futures Trading Commission v. Donald R. Wilson and DRW Investments, 13-civ-7884 (U.S. District Court, Southern District of New York, 2018) at 26 (Sullivan, an appeals court judge in the 2nd U.S. Circuit Court of Appeals, was sitting by designation in the U.S. District Court for the Southern District of New York).

5. Dick Bryan and Michael Rafferty, *Capitalism with Derivatives: A Political Economy of Financial Derivatives, Capital and Class* (London: Palgrave Macmillan, 2006); Stefano Pagliari, Lauren Phillips and Kevin Young, "The Financialization of Policy Preferences: Financial Asset Ownership, Regulation and Crisis Management," *Socio-Economic Review*, Vol. 18, No. 3 (July 2020), 655–680.

6. Peto v. Howell, 101 F.2d 353 (7th Circuit Court of Appeals, 1938). For the electricity trading, see remarks by Senator Diane Feinstein in *CFTC Regulation and Oversight of Derivatives: Hearing Before the Committee on Agriculture, Nutrition, and Forestry*, United States Senate, One Hundred Seventh Congress, second session, July 10, 2002 (Washington: Government Printing Office, 2003), 4, 5; David Ress, "California's Balance of Power, A Complex Juggling Act," *The Star Ledger* (Newark, New Jersey), January 24, 2001, 1.

7. *The Role of Market Speculation on Rising Oil and Gas Prices: A Need to Put the Cop Back on the Beat*, Staff Report, U.S. Senate Permanent Subcommittee on Investigations, June 27, 2006 (Washington: Government Printing Office, 2006), 1–2.

8. Shortly after the start of trading in "time contracts" or futures in grain on the Chicago Board of Trade, the Illinois legislature in 1868 banned short-selling grain for future delivery, but this was widely ignored as speculators that year realized that "in long buying … under skillful management … prices [were] unnaturally forced about their natural level, much to the disgust and pecuniary embarrassment of the short sellers" with three corners in wheat contracts, one in oats and two in corn. Alfred T. Andreas, *History of Chicago: from the earliest period to the present time* (Chicago; A.T. Andreas, 1882), Vol. 2, 362; "Dealing in fictitious farm products" had turned produce exchanges like the Chicago Mercantile Exchange, which started as a place where wholesalers could arrange a day's or week's supply of butter and eggs for their

grocer clients, into "a place of fixing prices ... where the initiated are able to secure great gain without performing any service for the community, but, on the contrary, destroy the prosperity of the cultivator," said Rep. William H. Hatch, a Democrat from Missouri who was chairman of the House Agriculture Committee, when proposing legislation in 1892 to end "this unnatural and vicious system," with a stiff tax on futures contracts and options. House Committee on Agriculture, "Dealing in Fictious Farm Products," House of Representatives Report No. 969, 52nd Congress, 1st Session (1892).

9. "Transactions on the New York Stock Exchange," *New York Times*, October 25, 1929, 42; "Dividends Announced," Ibid., 52. Follansbee was a particularly dramatic example, but not the only one where share prices plunged when news about the income a share might generate for a holder suggested prices in theory should rise or at least hold steady: what was happening, that is, was that people were buying and selling the market, not really shares in a company. So Norfolk and Western might report a 110% increase in trailing twelve month earnings on Black Thursday but its shares still fell seventeen percent by the of end the day on Black Tuesday, to $215; Atlas Powder Company might report a thirty-four percent increase in third quarter profits on October 25, 1929 but after the Black Monday and Black Tuesday, its share price was down thirty percent to $80. No news of any change in earnings, net worth or dividend payment plans had emerged for Allied Chemical and Dye Co, but it still saw the price of its shares fall twenty six percent to $210. "Transactions on the New York Stock Exchange," *New York Times*, October 25, 1929, 40 October 30, 1929, 31; "Atlas Powder Report," Ibid., October 26, 1929, 25; "Railroad Earnings," Ibid., October 30, 1929, 38.Whatever it was that people were buying and selling on October 25 was not what people sold and bought on October 29; it was much more about a view of a market than it was about a view about Allied Chemical or Atlas Powder or the Norfolk and Western.

10. Ludwig von Mises, *Human Action: A Treatise on Economics* (Auburn, Alabama: The Ludwig von Mises Institute, 1998 [first published 1949]), 392.

11. In re Indiana Farm Bureau Cooperative Association and Louis M. Johnston, Docket 75–14, Opinion and Order (Commodity

Futures Trading Commission, 1982), 31, https://www.cftc.gov/sites/default/files/idc/groups/public/@lrceacases/documents/ceacases/indiana-johnston-dec1982-9.pdf.

12. John Maynard Keynes, *The General Theory of Employment, Interest and Money* (New York: Harcourt Brace & Co., 1936), 161.

13. Roberts DeSaussure Newhall, *The Discourses of Jimmy* (Cincinnati: The Circular Advertising Co., 1908), 47, 60. "What's that got to do with the price of eggs" as a question testing an apparent non sequitur dates back to at least the 1890s, as in *History of the Class of 1895* (Princeton, N.J.: Privately printed, 1895), 70.

References

CFTC Regulation and Oversight of Derivatives: Hearing Before the Committee on Agriculture, Nutrition, and Forestry, United States Senate, One Hundred Seventh Congress, second session, July 10, 2002 (Washington: Government Printing Office, 2003)

Commodity Futures Trading Commission v. Donald R. Wilson and DRW Investments, 13-civ-7884 (U.S. District Court, Southern District of New York, 2018)

In re David G Henner, 30 Agricultural Decisions 1151

In re Indiana Farm Bureau Cooperative Association and Louis M. Johnston, Docket 75–14, Opinion and Order (Commodity Futures Trading Commission, 1982)

The Role of Market Speculation on Rising Oil and Gas Prices: A Need to Put the Cop Back on the Beat, Staff Report, U.S. Senate Permanent Subcommittee on Investigations, June 27 2006 (Washington: Government Printing Office, 2006)

Bryan, Dick and Michael Rafferty: *Capitalism with Derivatives: A Political Economy of Financial Derivatives, Capital and Class* (London: Palgrave Macmillan, 2006)

Friedman, Milton: *Capitalism and Freedom* (Chicago: University of Chicago Press, 1982 [first published 1962])

Keynes, John Maynard: *The General Theory of Employment, Interest and Money* (New York: Harcourt Brace & Co., 1936)

Pagliari, Stefano, Lauren Phillips and Kevin Young: "The Financialization of Policy Preferences: Financial Asset Ownership, Regulation and Crisis Management," *Socio-Economic Review*, Vol. 18, No. 3 (July 2020) 655–680

von Mises, Ludwig: *Human Action: A Treatise on Economics* (Auburn, Alabama: The Ludwig von Mises Institute, 1998 [first published 1949])

CHAPTER 2

Disconnections

Abstract The theatrics of the June 25, 1968 close of trading in the fresh egg futures market involved two steps: first, the clearing of the market by simultaneously buying all the wide ranging offers pending at the time, followed by a bid at the maximum price allowed by Chicago Mercantile Exchange rules. The market had been trading tentatively for a few weeks, poised to either rally or decline, in part because none of traders, including the author of the June 25 drama, David Henner, really understood what was happening with demand and supply of the underlying asset of this particular asset.

Keywords Futures markets · Derivative instruments · Artificial price · Price theory

Through the morning of June 25, 1968, the buying and selling of shell egg futures contracts had proceeded uncertainly, leaving the floor brokers plenty of time to contemplate implications of the latest of the intermittent $5/100$ths or $10/100$ths of a cent tick up or down. Then came the startling, sudden burst of activity at the close, when David Henner, who had not done anything for the three and a half hours the market had been open that day, called out that he would buy the board and then, as the closing bell sounded, bid the maximum allowed by Chicago Mercantile

D. Ress, *Market Manipulation and The Price of Eggs*, https://doi.org/10.1007/978-3-031-87171-9_2

11

Exchange rules—a limit-up 41.85 cents—for one last contract. It looked unreal to almost everyone, for it was out of step with the market trend, as Irving Manaster, a member of the Mercantile Exchange who had traded for his own account since 1941, would later testify. Manaster said he didn't jump to hit Henner's 41.85 cent bid, which would have represented an instantaneous paper profit of five percent, because "there wasn't enough time. Nobody knew what was going on." That bid, he added, was "completely out of line." When another floor broker, Marlowe King, after perhaps fifteen seconds of confusion jumped on Henner's bid, all Manaster could ruefully say was that "He is faster than me. I can't think that fast."[1]

In the seconds after Marlowe King and David Henner struck their 41.85 cent deal, floor broker John Hoekstra hastened to over to complain. He said he had "got stuck" with three stop loss orders—two from a client who wanted to close out open short contracts a November future at 40.5 cents and a third order to buy at 40.65 cents—and had been about to hit three of the bids posted on the shell egg futures ring's blackboard when Henner bought the board. Henner was "raiding the market," Hoekstra complained. In response, Henner handed over the tickets for three of the highest priced futures, including his 41.85 cent a dozen contract to buy 18,000 dozen eggs, and Hoekstra, satisfied (and, in fact, having done better for his clients) let the matter drop.[2]

Embedded in the 41.85 cent deal for the November future at the closing bell, then, was an almost automatic, nervous response of reflex—Manaster's that did not work in time and Marlowe King's that did. In addition, while it was a transaction that set a price, it did not end with a purchase: Henner did not end up with the contract he had bid for. Henner's own gesture—perhaps on reflex—to give away his three highest priced contracts, "[p]resumably in order to preserve Mr. Hoekstra's good will" seemed fishy to U.S. Department of Agriculture Judicial Officer Donald Campbell, one of several things in those moments at the close of trading in the egg futures ring that signaled something improper when Campbell revied that day's trading. While such courtesies to soothe the frictions and aggravations of competitive buying and selling were not unknown, if not common, Henner could have made his good will move without quite being quite so generous to Hoekstra's clients, Campbell noted. Turning over the 40.5 cent and two of the three 40.75 cent contracts Henner had acquired when he bought the board would also have allowed Hoesktra to fill the stop loss orders.

I would like to suggest that wheeling and dealing of exchange—bidding and offering in an open outcry market like the egg futures ring—can at times involve very common human experiences of, for instance, excitement and reflex, or an individual's calculation and game-playing. Reflex is one theory about what happened that June afternoon; one that challenges Campbell's interpretation of a market manipulation; games-playing might seem to confirm the judicial officer's finding. An exchange, too, can be about creating social connection: making peace, as with a potlach—or the handing over of some egg futures contracts. None of these, not reflex, nor game-playing nor gift fit in well with the theory of what was supposedly happening in the egg futures ring, or for that matter in any free, competitive market. As Department of Agriculture Judicial Officer Donald Campbell would comment, in the usual operation of a free market—in the way the shell egg futures market was supposed to operate:

> Both the buyers and sellers would be using their informed judgment as to supply and demand conditions *for eggs* that would exist four or five months later. If such buyers try to buy as cheaply as they can and such sellers try to sell as high as they can, the free forces of supply and demand on *the Exchange* as reflected by the trading activities of such buyers and sellers will result in a normal price.[3]

For most of that day, such informed judgment had required as much as thirty minutes for the floor brokers to react to the last deal struck, time during which, at least in theory, they would be reweighing their thoughtful and informed analyses of likely supply and demand for eggs five months in the future. The bids and offers of futures market speculators and hedgers, or so the officials who ran commodity exchanges had been telling the public since the late nineteenth century, sent an important signal about prices of farm products, a guide to farmers about how much to plant (or how many pullets to buy for their hen houses) while helping wholesalers, millers and other processes manage inventories and draft buying and reselling plans.

Not one of the brokers in the egg futures pit was actually buying or selling eggs, however. They did not raise eggs, they had no place to store eggs and they had no network of customers who wanted eggs for breakfast or grocers who wanted to market eggs. They were buying and selling contracts to supply or acquire eggs at various times in the future. These were contracts for notional eggs that, moreover, they could unwind by simply finding a counter-party for mirror-image deal. These were, that is, notional contracts for notional sales of eggs. In June 1968, growers and wholesalers actually involved in the egg trade held a grand total of four contracts conditionally promising to buy eggs at a specific price and fifty-five to sell eggs.[4]

The Mercantile Exchange, in fact, no longer traded real eggs, and had only introduced the November shell egg future contract (as well as the July, October and December contracts) that year—previously, only a January and a September contract traded.[5] As traders felt their way with these new contracts, the spread between the November future's price and the average farm price in June, which the U.S.D.A. estimated at 30.3 cents, and the July future, at 30.5 cents was quite wide: 10.45 cents a dozen; at the same time in June, 1969, the spread was 2.3 cents.[6]

Such disconnection between what is traded in a derivatives market— the contracts—and the underlying asset—eggs, in this case—is why futures markets (and like the secondary markets in stocks and bonds) can be useful places to ask if, when or how the price of something might be unreal. Ironically, Henner's 41.85 cent a dozen bid for eggs to be delivered at the end of November was not that far off the average price farmers received for their eggs that month—it was 41.9 cents a dozen, U.S. Department of Agriculture statisticians calculated—but the price of the November futures contract when it expired was much lower: 39.25 cents, even though theory, futures and cash prices are to converge when the contract expires.[7] If Henner's 41.85 cent bid seemed disconnected from the cash market at the time he called it out (though none of the other traders likely would have thought that disconnection at all relevant) the price of the November contract at expiry was clearly not connected at all to the price of eggs.

In the traders' confusion at the closing bell on June 25, what struck them most immediately was that Henner's 41.85 cents was out of line with the prices for November futures contracts earlier that day; including the eight contracts Henner acquired when he bought the board just seconds before). Still later, they would also see that the 41.85 cent deal also was out of line with prices quoted at that moment for October and December egg futures contracts; all three should have been moving roughly in tandem, at least (once again) so the theory of futures markets contended.

For some forty minutes before Henner bought the board and then called out his 41.85 cent bid, nobody else in the egg futures ring wanted to move from the price that two of the floor brokers had agreed was 40.30 cents a dozen. Neither the low asking price of 40.20 cents posted on the blackboard nor the high of 41.30 seemed right. For those forty minutes, the market's actors were satisfied that 40.3 cents a dozen was the right price for notional eggs in November, five months in the future. An equilibrium, and an unusually stable one for a futures market, had emerged in a marketplace where what traders usually wanted to see was ever-changing prices, since guessing correctly on these changes was where their profits came. In the confusion that then followed Henner's 41.85 bid, it still took time—a brief time, to be sure—for any of the brokers to get over their shock. When Marlowe King did and hit Henner's bid, 41.85 cents became the new and much higher price, real or not. Once King struck his deal, it seemed an obvious move for a sell-side trader, even though, until he did, it was not at all obvious to anyone else in the egg futures ring. Missing the chance for a quick (if paper) profit, was why long-time exchange member Manaster would lament his own, slower reflex. It was why floor broker John Hoekstra, when Henner's bid kept him from a chance to fill three orders would complain of unfair dealing.[8] Was the real price for those notional eggs to be delivered in five months' time, then, closer to the 40.30 cents everyone had been content with or the 41.85 cents a dozen contract that Henner was perfectly happy to give away rather than keep for himself?

If Henner had not given his 41.85 cent contract to buy eggs in November away, he could have canceled it simply by successfully offering a contract to sell November eggs. The money that changed hands for such contracts—and not between buyer and seller, but between broker and a Mercantile Exchange clearing house member firm—was fraction of the notional price of those eggs: 6.6% in the case of Henner's and King's deal. What was out of whack, in Manaster's view, was nothing to do with the price of eggs but rather the gap between the 41.85 cents for the November contract, the 40.2 to 41.3 that Henner had seconds earlier paid for November contracts when he bought the board and the 38.25 cents for October contracts and 39.50 for Decembers.[9]

Some basics and some market jargon might help here. Buying and selling do not have their ordinary meaning in a market for derivative instruments. On June 25, 1968 Henner's bid was actually an offer to sell a contract, in this case to buy eggs five months in the future that he had no intention of actually purchasing. He was dealing in a contract, not eggs—the eggs would not be laid for at least sixteen to twenty weeks. Doing this, Henner was going long, or taking a long position, market terms that will make it somewhat easier to follow what is going on. When Henner bought the board—that is, agreeing to buy the variously-priced contracts for the sale of eggs in November—and struck his 41.85 cent deal with Marlowe King, he was adding to his long position. When Henner called out his 41.85 cent bid, he was not really bidding to buy eggs in November. Instead, he was offering a contract to buy eggs. This complicates Campbell's test of the reality of a price, that a true price is the result of trading where a buyer always seeks a low price and the seller a high one. Looked at as a bidder to buy eggs in November, Henner should have been seeking the lowest price he could; looked at as the offeror of a contract, he was, appropriately enough, seeking a high price.

Futures markets deal in large, if notional, volumes, meanwhile. By the end of the day on June 25, Henner's move to buy the board and then pay the maximum price for that final contract amounted to a conditional promise to buy 14.7 million eggs at the end of November, an apparent commitment of nearly $500,000. When Henner bought the board and did his final 41.85 cent deal, he had already accumulated fifty-nine November shell egg futures contracts he had already nailed down at prices ranging from 37.70 cents a dozen to 41 cents.[10] The 68 contracts Henner had when King hit that last bid were for a total of 1,224,000 dozen eggs; roughly as many as farmers in the major producing state of Ohio marketed in an average month and more than the monthly average from all but six states.[11] The supply supposedly in the egg futures market, assuming everybody was trading eggs, was orders of magnitude larger than the real eggs that could ever come to market.

When Marlowe King, on the other side of the 41.85 cent deal, bought the contract Henner was selling, he was thereby conditionally promising to sell 18,000 dozen notional eggs for 41.85 cents a dozen. In the market jargon, this was a short position. For King, that conditional sale at 41.85 cents, some 1.55 cents above what had until then been the day's high, would have looked like an easy profit on Henner's inexplicable move—so easy that floor broker Irving Manaster could only bemoan that fact that he was seconds too slow to grab the gain for himself.

A few seconds was all it took, however. They were not real eggs, after all. None of the 216,000 eggs that Henner's 41.85 cent a dozen deal said he would buy had even been laid—they would not even begin to be laid for another four to four and a half months. Henner expected to cancel the deal at some point before November with a short: a promise to sell 216,000 notional eggs; in the event, he simply gave the contract away to Hoekstra so that, in Judicial Officer Campbell's view, it was not a completed transaction, and the bid was not a real price. Henner did close his other long contracts, months later. His intention in going long was to unwind those notional contracts with higher-priced shorts—contracts, never to be exercised, to sell notional eggs for more than his initial notional contracts had promised to pay for eggs. The difference would be his profit. On the other side of the deal, Marlowe King had no eggs to sell, since none of the eggs in the 18,000 dozen he said he would sell for 41.85 cents had been laid, and he had no way of knowing if he could acquire 216,000 eggs in late November, and in fact no intention of actually selling any real eggs. Like Henner, he expected to cancel the sale promised in his contract with an offsetting contract to supply eggs—eggs that also did not exist. In Henner's case, the 216,000 eggs in his 41.85 cents a dozen deal came on top of the fifty-nine contract long position he had begun assembling in January at prices between 37 cents and 39.95 as well as the eight contracts he acquired when he bought the board a minute earlier. Henner and the counterparties to his futures contracts had, in effect created 14.7 million virtual eggs out of thin air, in the expectation that those virtual eggs would vanish before any real eggs would ever actually be exchanged.

The qualifiers "notional," "conditional" or "supposedly" matter. For there was another promise here: the promise made by a market, in this case the Chicago Mercantile Exchange, of a never-ending competition between buyers and sellers that ensured that a deal could always be agreed, even if perhaps a profit might not. In the same way, shorts, like Marlowe King in this case, expected that they, too, would be able to unwind their positions with matching long contracts. Even for those dealers in real eggs who used futures to hedge against the risk that the eventual actual price of eggs might fall to a level where they would lose money (if in the unlikely event they were farmers or farmer cooperatives) or rise to a point that would cut their margins (if they were shippers or wholesalers) almost never took delivery or supplied a commodity. Although a promise to buy, a long position, could in theory be fulfilled by taking delivery of the commodity (or of warehouse receipts for the commodity) or a short by delivering real eggs or warehouse receipts in any futures market was in practice almost always—roughly in ninety-nine percent of cases—erased by a promise to sell (for the November shell egg future it would be 53,740 contracts out of 54,116 traded, or 99.3%).[12] Finding eggs, or wheat, or corn or cotton that met the precise quantity and quality measures specified in a futures contract, shipping the commodity to one of a small number of exchange-designated warehouses detailed in a futures contract's specifications and certifying that the goods met the contract standards (or negotiating a discount or premium if they did not) was too cumbersome a process to bother with in most cases. Several of the other Commodity Exchange Authority cases of market manipulation, in fact, involved situations where traders with short positions at a contract expiry who were unable to find anything to deliver on the cash market had to cover their shorts with long contracts after a sudden, sharp price spike as a market corner became evident.

In theory, a futures contract was a kind of insurance. A producer—an egg farmer, perhaps—could take out a short position on the theory that if cash prices fell, it would be possible to offset that decline by unwinding the short at a profit. (The scale of any single farmer's operations made this impractical, since the future contract's 600 cases of 30 dozen eggs was more than the any but the largest operation of the day could deliver in the ten-day period for delivery specified by the contract.[13]) A shipper or wholesaler seeking to hedge the risk of a rise in cash prices could mitigate the impact of that when unwinding a long futures position. Because of the tiny downpayment, the margin, required to deal in futures and the easy way of unwinding a contract, the insurance such hedges provided was in theory a low cost was of shifting risk to speculators. In fact, speculators, rather than the producers or users of goods were to free market enthusiasts like the economist Ludwig von Mises, "The driving force of the market process," for "Quicker of apprehension and farther-sighted than other men," speculators in commodity and money markets "circumscribe the orbit within which definite minor tasks can be entrusted to the manager's discretion …it is vain to cite the honest corporation manager and his well-tried efficiency."[14] Or, as the economist Frank Knight had noted, While the producers—farmers or miners, say—and users of any particular commodity may know more about demand and supply than a speculator, the speculator "gains an enormous advantage from the sheer magnitude or breadth of the scope of his operations." For "where a single flour miller or cotton spinner would be in the market once, the speculator enters it hundreds or thousands of times, and his errors in judgment must show a correspondingly stronger tendency to cancel out and leave him a constant and predictable return on his operations."[15] What Henner and King felt in June (not necessarily out of an in-depth knowledge) about eggs that would not be laid for many months was, in theory, a perfectly legitimate way to guide decisions about how many hens a farmer would feed that autumn or what a grocer might order.

Speculation in derivatives was (and is) a relatively low cost effort, at least compared to the cost of, for instance, setting up and running an operation that could produce 216,000 eggs for delivery in the final ten days of a month.[16] That's because the financial commitment involved in buying or selling a futures contract at the time was just a $500 margin payment—or, more usually, a debit to a traders' established account with the Mercantile Exchange clearing house. For a $4,500 debit to a clearing house account totaling $260,530, Henner was speculating that he could sell the nine contracts for 162,000 dozen eggs that he had acquired by buying the board and striking his final deal a contract for more than the $58,590 the contracts supposedly committed him to pay. The amounts involved were apparently trivial enough that he simply gave three of the nine contracts he acquired that day to John Hoekstra after Hoekstra complained of unfair dealing: the gesture that, or so Judicial Officer Campbell argued, was another bit of evidence that Henner had forced a false price on the market. When twenty days later, Henner sold nine contracts at prices from 41.85 cents to 42.25 cents he would have realized between $67,889 as much as $68,833; this amounts to a return of at least 15.9% over twenty days on the face value of his contracts, given that some of these sales closed longs he had acquired for even lower prices than his June 25 deals.[17]

In a commodity futures market, moreover, for all that, as the economist L. Dee Belveal would write in one of his several textbooks on commodity futures trading, "Supply and demand stand eyeball-to-eyeball in the pits and rings, in the form of orders to buy and sell for future delivery," traders do not really do that.[18] (Belveal would testify on Henner's behalf during the Commodity Exchange Authority investigation of his egg futures trading.) The deal Henner and King struck, like every other deal on every other commodity exchange, went to clearing house. Henner, if the price of the November future rose to the point where he could make money on his 41.85 cent deal would not have to confront a losing Marlow King in order buy an offsetting contract from King to liquidate his open long position. He would simply have to complete the sale of a short contract to anyone willing to buy it and settle with the clearing house. King would never have to deal with Henner again because all he needed to do was to show the clearing house he had the long contract that canceled his short. Since the buyer and seller of a futures contract take their profits, or their lumps, away from one another, and because they can make their easy-to-erase commitments to buy or sell commodities for a fraction of the cash outlay the contracts represent they do not have much at stake at the moment they strike a deal.

The numbers worked differently for the growers and wholesalers dealing in actual eggs. Farm prices for eggs through the winter and spring of 1968 averaged 29.6 cents a dozen, down 1.6 cents from the 1967 average, which was the lowest since the end of the Second World War. Despite a slight, 0.6% increase in the number of eggs brought to the market, growers' income fell 5.7% in the first half of 1968. A near doubling of the stockpile of unsold eggs in the first months of 1968 along with a two percent increase in egg production meant the supply of eggs for the U.S. domestic market (taking out military use and eggs meant for hatching chickens) was 5.5% higher in early 1968.[19] But the ratcheting down of farm prices for eggs, driven by an eight day stretch in late December 1967 to early January 1968 trading when one trader's accumulation of a large short position in the Chicago Mercantile Exchange egg pit had forced prices down by 10 cents a dozen, looked to National Egg Company general manager Jerry Faulkner like manipulation—especially when he tried bidding for two contracts in a effort to stop the price slide but was unable to complete a deal. Faulkner, who handled eggs for several large Georgia and Alabama producers, was one of the few traders in the egg futures market trying to hedge against a decline in cash prices: most growers operated on too small a scale for this. Everette Harris, president of the Chicago Mercantile Exchange, brushed off Faulkner's concern, saying the exchange was a free market and "free markets rectify these things rapidly." The market, it seemed, knew better than National Egg what the price should be: "A decline in prices should be effective in eliminating the surplus which still exists in eggs," Harris told Faulkner.[20]

The sharp drop in the November future at this time led Henner to experiment with going long—that is, responding to a low price in the way that, as Judicial Officer Campbell might have put it—a rational buyer, ever seeking the cheapest price might do. In the event, in January 1968, after the bear raid that Faulkner had complained off and that Harris had shrugged off, Henner, who would later testify that he did not usually play the long side of the market, did just that with four contracts, the first at 38 cents, followed by three others as prices dipped to 37 cents—a significant share of the twenty-nine November futures traded that month; while Henner's trading activity later would account for only a tiny share of egg futures pit volume, the other traders were aware that he had entered market early, and, unusually for him, as a long.[21]

But the price of the future did not rise, and he unwound this position at a slight loss in early February shorts at 37.50 and 37.75. He tested the water again in February and March, this time unwinding his longs at slight profits. It was with a dip in April to 37 cents that he moved aggressively to build his long, with a purchase of 28 contracts, adding to this through April, May and June even as prices increased—and as it happened, pulling up farm prices. By early June, the future was trading up by about a cent from its January level, farm prices were up about 7/10ths cent from their early 1968 lows.[22]

It was not just the possibility of buying at a low price that had attracted Henner to plunge in so dramatically on the long side of the market on April 16. (Henner had never bought more than nine November futures at a time before this.)[23] While the U.S. Department of Agriculture report on the numbers of hens laying eggs, some 320 million, up two percent from the previous year looked bearish, suggesting a larger than usual supply of eggs, Henner thought the large percentage of older and less productive hens and a five percent decline in the number of younger replacement hens added to flocks meant late autumn would see tightening supply. Confirmation seemed to come from a U.S. Department of Agriculture report of a fifteen percent decline in chicks hatched in the first quarter of the year—that is, pullets that would begin laying eggs by the start of summer—as well as a one-third decline in pullets less than three months old and a twenty-two percent decline in the number of eggs in incubators, the hens that would begin laying eggs at the end of the summer.[24] The message seemed clear: Older hens produce fewer eggs while the younger ones would be molting, and not laying eggs until their new feathers came in, On top of this, the egg price to feed price ratio, which slid from 8.2 in to 7.3 in 1968, far below the 9.5 to 11.5 ratios from the high farm price of eggs in the early to mid-1960s, suggested growers would set out fewer hens in order to hold down costs.[25] In fact, growers, logically enough, bought fewer pullets, 280 million as of January 1968 compared to 283 million in January 1967. The U.S. Department of Agriculture report of a fifteen percent decline in chicks hatched in the first quarter of the year—that is, pullets that would begin laying eggs by the start of summer and through the rest of the year, including November—as well as a one-third decline in pullets less than three months old and a twenty-two percent decline in the number of eggs in incubators, the hens that would begin laying eggs at the end of the summer, continuing through November and into the new year, confirmed this read. Henner thought he saw a late autumn supply that would be even smaller than usual: enough so that he expected egg prices would rise to levels never seen before.[26]

Encouraged by the U.S. Department of Agriculture analysts' view (echoing the hopes of hard-pressed growers) that prices in the second half of the year would be "moderately to substantially above year ago levels," Henner had decided that sometime between mid-July and the November 22 expiry of the November shell egg future, the rest of the players in the futures market would see this, too. He decided that they would bid the price of the November future up to 50 cents or 58 cents.[27] This was an extremely bullish view: the future had never traded above 46 cents, and that was back in 1955 while the high for the 1960s was barely 40 cents.[28] At the lower end of that range, he was looking at a profit of roughly $110,000 on the face value of $421,000 worth of futures—contracts that had actually required a margin payment of $29,500.[29] Even when the Chicago wholesale price for eggs peaked in September at 43.85 cents, the November future never breached the 45 cent level and it closed at 39.25 cents on expiry.[30]

Henner kept buying, in small amounts of one to no more than seven contracts in any one day, building up a long position of 55 contracts by the end of April. He did nothing for another three weeks, before buying two contracts, at 40.50 cents a dozen; he sold two at 42 two weeks later, At the lower end of that range, he was looking at a profit of roughly $110,000 on the face value of $421,000 worth of futures—contracts that only had required a margin payment of $29,500.[31]

While other traders did not see what Henner thought he saw in the statistics on laying hens, pullets, hatcheries and egg price to feed price ratio, what they heard about May shipments, which ended up slipping to 108,000 cases from 117,000 the year before, as well as the still steeper drop in June, which cases shipments fell to 154,0000 from 265,000 sparked what was for Henner only a frustratingly tentative rally.[32] The price of November futures rose to end the day at 42.30 cents a dozen on June 11. At this point, though, most traders in shell egg futures began, if somewhat uncertainly, to feel the shell egg futures market had got a bit ahead of itself. Prices slipped steadily to close at 39.50 cents on June 21, a Friday. Over the weekend, the sense that this, too, had gone too far grew and on Monday, June 24, the November future tentatively edged higher, to close at 40 cents. Henner stepped in at this point, buying three contracts at 40 cents.[33] "It was a little bit of a change and they were getting a little bit of umph," as the economist Dee Belveal told a Commodity Exchange Authority hearing on Henner's egg futures trading.[34]

With this in mind—that new if uncertain upward momentum—what Henner did at the close the next day, June 25, by buying the board and then bidding the highest allowed price for one final November future seemed clear enough to Arthur J. Parz, a member of the Chicago Mercantile Exchange and a floor broker for about 15 years. As he explained at a Commodity Exchange Authority hearing, he "thought Henner was trying to bull the market on June 25th, hoping that November eggs would continue to go higher." "Now, if a person is a speculator and he buys, why is he buying?" the attorney for the authority asked. "Because he thinks that the price of November eggs is going to go higher," Parz replied. "Is that bulling the market, so to speak?" the attorney asked. "At this particular time, yes, it is," Parz replied. To "bull the market," neither man needed to explain to a market regulator like Judicial Officer Campbell, meant to make progressively higher bids for a particular futures contract to attract others' attention and spark additional bids to drive prices still higher, so that speculator bulling the market could cash in earlier contracts with lower bid prices at a profit.[35]

At the moment that Henner called out his 41.85 cent bid, convinced that the price of the November future would rise still farther, it is important to remember that "the actual information as to the supply and demand conditions for eggs in November will not be known for four or five months," Judicial Officer Campbell commented, as he reviewed the hearing record.[36] Even when the Chicago wholesale price for actual eggs peaked in September at 43.85 cents, the November future never breached the 46 cent level and it closed at 38.90 bid, 40.45 asked, an unusually wide spread in a thinly traded market where the handful of deals struck ranged between 38.75 cents and 40.45 cents, exactly the kind of large range that Judicial Officer Campbell found suspicious with the trading on June 25.[37] While "[e]xpert witnesses could always be found to testify that, in their opinion, the November futures price on June 25 was too low and other expert witnesses could always be found to testify that, in their opinion, the price was too high," Campbell added, the best 'expert opinion' … as to what the normal November futures price should be on June 25 is the price established by the free forces of supply and demand on the Exchange, i.e., by buyers trying to buy as cheaply as they can and sellers trying to sell as high as they can.[38]

That dynamic of trying to buy cheaply and sell dearly mattered, Campbell said, because the futures market was the way the egg market discovered where prices for eggs were going; it was, he wrote, the most important function of a futures market.[39] In theory, what futures price did helped growers determine how many hens to set out and feed and whole-salers to think about how many eggs their retailer customers' customers would buy. Henner's dealing, he felt, could do so even though Henner was not at any point considering buying or selling eggs. He was looking at the determinants of egg prices (if not quite with the expert eye he claimed to have) to lay a bet in the futures market. With his focus on the autumn, there would have been no way to be in the market for real eggs at the time Henner acted: any eggs that changed hands in April, May or June would have long since spoiled by the July to November time Henner expected egg prices to rise.

But the egg business was changing. As farmers expanded the scale of their egg operations, with the number of laying hens up two percent from already high levels of 1967, confounding the conventional wisdom (in a fairly typical pattern for farm products) that soft prices should lead producers to bring less of their product to the market, growers also were introducing a new technique. They kept older hens laying at high rates through the usual late autumn slump in egg production by force-molting them—denying them food for several days—several weeks earlier. This new practice simulated the natural process of shedding and regrowth of feathers, which paused and then restarted egg production at a high level. Force-molting was an answer to the problem of what had been a seasonal drop egg production in the autumn, when even the youngest and most productive hens began shedding—the seasonal supply variation that Henner hoped to profit from. What Henner missed in his reading of the U.S.D.A. April report on the egg-laying flock and hatchery trends was the note that growers' traditional practice of culling of their older, and normally less productive hens, was moderating: while "this year's flock contains an unusually large number of replacements added in the spring 1967" that "are now reaching the end of their laying cycle which would normally be followed by heavy culling …the rate of culling may be tempered somewhat by a higher rate of forced molting."[40] In fact, growers had 260 million hens laying eggs as of October 1968, well above the 236 million in October 1967.[41]

Did the other traders see this? It is not clear that they were looking. Arthur J. Parz, who had been trading futures for fifteen years, told Commodity Exchange Authority officials that he could not say whether the "price of 41.85 was or was not realistic to the actual market conditions relative to November eggs at the time they were to be delivered in November." Still, he said, Henner's 41.85 cent bid "out of proportion completely" because it priced the November future nearly four cents higher than the October contract, well above the 2.5 cent spread it had been trading at.[42] Of the twenty-three contracts brokers other than Henner bought that day, thirteen were at prices below the 40.2 cent low asking price posted when he bought the board: everyone else around the shell egg futures pit, that is, was poised to deal at prices well below the deal Henner and King struck.[43] Why then, Campbell asked, would Henner say he would pay so much more? "A normal November shell egg futures price on June 25 would be based on the actions of buyers on the Exchange trying to buy as cheaply as they can and sellers trying to sell as high as they can," Campbell noted.[44]

Henner would say his 41.85 cent bid was at that instant exactly the price he needed to complete one final deal that day: a free market balancing of that passing moment's actual demand and supply for the November contract. Other traders in the egg futures pit said it was an unreal price, out of step with the market consensus of the value of a November egg future, though as the range of bids on the egg futures pit blackboard when Henner bought the board suggests, there really was no consensus. Dee Belveal, the economist Henner called on to help with his defense against charge he had violated federal law, said variously (and sometimes within minutes) that the 41.85 cents a dozen price reflected the real value of the November future, that it was atrocious, that it was an important valid signal to other buyers and sellers of futures contracts and that it was a mistake, eventually corrected by the usual operation of a free market in a reaction that demonstrated that the ideal free market worked. U.S. Department of Agriculture Judicial Officer Donald Campbell would conclude Henner had forced false price on the market to signal to other speculators that prices were about to rally.

Without Henner's "intentional action to raise the closing price" by "intentionally paying more than he had to," Campbell said the closing price on June 25 would have been about 40.20 or 40.30, or 1.55 to 1.65 cents lower. Even though, once Marlowe King agreed to accept Henner's 41.85 cents bid, the two traders had concluded exactly what conventional analysis accepted as the determinant of real prices, the real value of goods and services: the agreement of willing buyer and willing seller, Campbell held that the drama Henner staged—buying the board and then making that limit up, 41.85 cent a dozen bid—was disconnected with anything that was going on with the supply of or demand for eggs, or for that matter with futures contracts for eggs, which were not quite the same thing. It was, that is, a false price.

NOTES

1. In re Henner, 1186, 1215.
2. In re Henner at 1162–1163. The offers on the board were for one contact at 40.2 cents, one at 40.25 cents, one at 40.50 cents, three at 40.75 cents, one at 41 cents and one at 41.3 cents, In re Henner 1191.
3. In re Henner, 1194 (emphasis in the original).
4. Table 20. Annual average of midmonth and monthend long and short commitments of reporting and nonreporting traders, principal markets, *Commodity Futures Statistics* (Department of Agriculture, 1970), 52.
5. Bob Tamarkin, *The Merc: The Emergence of a Global Financial Powerhouse* (New York: HarperBusiness, 1993), 172; Table 17, Closing prices on principal markets by future, semimonthly, *Commodity Futures Statistics* (July 1966–July 1967), 39.
6. Table 17, Closing prices on principal markets by future, semimonthly, *Commodity Futures Statistics* (July 1967–July 1968), 39; Table 16. Closing prices on principal markets by future, semimonthly, *Commodity Futures Statistics* (July 1968–July 1969), 42; U.S. Department of Agriculture Economic Research Service, *Poultry and Egg Situation*, November 1968, 4.
7. Poultry and Egg Situation at a Glance, *Poultry and Egg Situation*, February 1969, p. 3; Table 16. Closing prices on principal markets by future, semimonthly, *Commodity Futures Statistics, no. 444* (July 1968–July 1969), 42.
8. In re Henner at 1162–1163.
9. Ibid., 1171, 1215.

10. Ibid., at 1165–1166.
11. Calculated from Table 25, "Eggs Marketed Under Contract," in Poultry, *Census of Agriculture* 1969, Vol. 5, Part 7, p. 47, 1969.
12. Calculated from Table 19 "Contracts settled by delivery in each contract market, by future" *Commodity Futures Statistics* (July 1968–July 1969), 49 and Table 4 "monthly volume of trading in principal markets, by future" *Commodity Futures Statistics* (July 1967–July 1968), 14 and *Commodity Futures Statistics* (July 1968–July 1969), 15.
13. Even after the dramatic decline in the number of egg growers and expansion and mechanization of the remaining operations in the mid 1960s, monthly production at the summertime peak in 1969 averaged a mean of just under 13,000 eggs (1,080 dozen); with an average of 686 laying hens on 445,519 farms, and with each hen laying 18.9 eggs a month, egg production was still on a fairly small scale. calculated from the Census of Agriculture, 1969, Table 20 "Livestock, Poultry, Livestock and Poultry Products, 21; Poultry and Egg Situation, September 1969, 2.
14. Von Mises, *Human Action*, 325, 704.
15. Frank Knight, *Risk, Uncertainty and Profit* (Boston: Houghton Mifflin, 1921), 256.
16. In 2024, it can cost more than $1 million to set up a operation for 18,000 hens. David Ress, "Va. Farmers Find New Egg Market," *Richmond (Va.) Times-Dispatch*, April 15, 2024, D1.
17. Buying the board meant one contact at 40.2 nts, one at 40.25 cents, one at 40.50 cents, three at 40.75 cents, one at 41 cents and one at 41.3 cents, with the 41.85 cent contract, these represent a face value of $58,590. Selling eight contracts at 41.85 cents and one at 42.25 cents yields the $67,889; one contact at 41.85cents and eight at 42.25 cents the $68,833.
18. L. Dee Belveal, *Charting Commodity Market Price Behavior* (Wilmette, Illinois: Commodity Press, 1969), x.
19. U.S. Department of Agriculture, *Poultry and Egg Situation* (November 1968), 4, 16, 18.
20. "Inquiry in Chicago Egg Trading Urged after Wide Price Swings," *New York Times*, January 8, 1968: 43.
21. Table 4 "monthly volume of trading in principal markets, by future" *Commodity Futures Statistics* (July 1967–July 1968), 14; In re Henner 1187.

22. In re Henner, 1165–1166.

23. Ibid., 1165.

24. *Poultry and Egg Situation* April 1968, 5, 9, 10.

25. Ibid., 10; Ibid., November 1968, 20.

26. Ibid., April 1968, 5, 9, 10.

27. In re Henner, 1176.

28. Arnold B. Larson, "Price Prediction on the egg Futures Market," *Food Research Institute Studies*, Vol 7 (1967), 60.

29. Calculated from the listing of Henner's purchases reported by In re Henner, 1165–1166. The average price was 39.67 cents, a rise to a price of 50 cents would represent a roughly 26 per cent increase in face value to $531,000. If the futures price had risen that far (it did not) Henner would have received $17 for every dollar he had actually put down in margin payments.

30. *Poultry and Egg Situation*, June 1969, 28; "Prices of Commodity Futures Are Listed," *New York Times*, September 20, 1968, 77; November 21, 1968, 64; Table 16 "Closing Prices on Principal Markets, by future," *Commodity Futures Statistics* (July 1968–July 1969), 42.

31. Calculated from the listing of Henner's purchases reported by In re Henner, 1165–1166. The average price was 39.67 cents, a rise to a price of 50 cents would represent a roughly 26% increase in face value to $531,000. If the futures price had risen that far (it did not) Henner would have received $17 for every dollar he had actually put down in margin payments.

32. *Poultry and Egg Situation*, June 1969, 30.

33. In re Henner, 1166.

34. Ibid., 1176.

35. Ibid. 1186, 1190–1191.

36. Ibid., 1199.

37. *Poultry and Egg Situation*, June 1969, 28; "Prices of Commodity Futures Are Listed," *New York Times*, September 20, 1968, 77; November 21, 1968, 64.

38. In re Henner, 1199.

39. Ibid., 1241.

40. *Poultry and Egg Situation*, April 1968, 5.

41. *Poultry and Egg Situation*, November 1968, 20.

42. In re Henner, 1216, 1173.

43. Ibid., 1163.

44. Ibid., 1194.

REFERENCES

Census of Agriculture, 1969 (U.S. Census Bureau)

Commodity Futures Statistics (1966–1967) (1967–1968) and (1968–1969) (Washington: U.S. Department of Agriculture)

In re David G Henner, 30 Agricultural Decisions 1151

Poultry and Egg Situation (U.S. Department of Agriculture) April 1968, November 1968, February 1969, June 1969

Belveal, L. Dee: *Charting Commodity Market Price Behavior* (Wilmette, Illinois: Commodity Press, 1969)

Knight, Frank: *Risk, Uncertainty and Profit* (Boston: Houghton Mifflin, 1921)

Larson, Aaron "Price Prediction on the Egg Futures Market," *Food Research Institute Studies*, Vol 7 (1967), 49–64

Tamarkin, Bo: *The Merc: The Emergence of a Global Financial Powerhouse* (New York: HarperBusiness, 1993)

von Mises, Ludwig: *Human Action: A Treatise on Economics* (Auburn, Alabama: The Ludwig von Mises Institute, 1998 [first published 1949])

CHAPTER 3

Chart Watching

Abstract There were three signs of price artificiality in the egg futures market on June 25, 1968. The first was the daily price variation of the November shell egg future was far larger than the normal pattern. The second, that the spreads between the October and November and the November and December contracts were far wider than normal. The third was when Henner acted and when he did not. For regulators, it was Henner's focus on marking a particular price—the maximum permitted daily—that was key to motive. This, they argued, was to create a pattern that would signal to chart-watching technical analysts (really, amateur speculators) that a rally was about to happen. It was these patterns that proved the price was artificial, and that artificiality with that intent that showed market manipulation, in the regulators' analysis.

Keywords Futures markets · Artificial price · Market manipulation · Regulation

David Henner's fifty-nine contract long position in the November shell egg future on the morning of June 25 gave him "an obvious motive for wanting to raise the closing price of November shell egg futures ... the full two cents permitted by the Exchange rules," Judicial Officer Donald Campbell noted. Barely above water at the June 24 close, Henner would

D. Ress, *Market Manipulation and The Price of Eggs*, https://doi.org/10.1007/978-3-031-87171-9_3

have lost money if prices of November futures slid as, in the absence of a strong upward move that day, they seemed poised to do, at least in the eyes of a school of speculators who saw in their charts of price movements which way a market was going, Campbell had calculated.[1] A drop in the future would have required Henner to supplement the margin he had deposited when buying those contracts, but his 41.85 cent bid, by boosting the day's average price by somewhere between 0.7 and 0.8 cents a dozen translated a credit of somewhere between $7,434 and $8,493—funds he could draw upon after the market closed as his margin for future trades.[2]

Beyond that immediate risk was another motive: Henner's belief that he knew better than the others where the price of the November future was headed, if only he could convince everyone else to see. If nobody else saw this in the U.S.D.A. reports that Henner seems to have been misreading, Henner, or so Judicial Officer Campbell concluded, figured they would see it in the charts of price trends that so many market players tracked.

Campbell built his argument that David Henner's last second 41.85 cents bid for a single November shell egg futures contract was an artificial price on three separate analyses. Two were tests of artificiality that many economists and most regulators had employed for decades, by asking whether a given price was out of line with other but related prices. The third test asked a question that was less typical: why had Henner, in his role as a buyer of notional eggs, not acted when the price was lower earlier in the day? All of these tests melded two issues: whether a price was artificial and if so whether that was the result of a specific intention to create a false price.

One of Campbell's tests, then, was that the normal daily range for the November contract was narrow; normal price discovery in the shell egg futures market did not involve dramatic, one-day moves. On 205 of the 212 days the November shell egg future traded, the daily price range was no more than one-fifth of a cent—far less, that is, than the increase Henner's last second, 41.85 bid; far less, in fact than the range of offers on the egg futures ring blackboard when Henner bought the board. The trading pattern before Henner bought the board and called out his final bid had been within that normal range and reflected a general sense of uncertainty about whether it was headed up or down after what chart-watchers would have seen as the confusing signal of the prior week's tentative reversal of what had looked like a downward trend.[3]

A second test was that trading in other shell egg futures—those for notional delivery in October and December—had not moved in tandem with Henner's final deals. These futures had advanced only slightly, as had the November before Henner's final bid.[4] The October future had started at a typical 1.95 cent discount to November on June 25, but ended at a 3.7 cent spread, as its price remained within a narrow range of six-tenths of a cent and rose only three-tenths of a cent. The pattern was similar for the December future. It opened at a 0.35 cent discount to November, again a fairly typical difference, but Henner's last second move generated a 2.35 cent spread. The October-to-November and November-to-December spreads returned to the more normal levels on June 26 and remained there through the summer.[5]

Spreads can signal something unusual in a futures market, where a common price pattern is what traders call "contango"—the notion that the prices for futures contracts in distant months should exceed the price of nearer month and cash market spot prices. Traders and market analysts generally view this pattern as a normal one because it reflects the cost of storing a commodity until delivery, as well as the premium due for taking a larger risk of being wrong about the eventual spot price as more and more time passes. (This is much like the idea that a normal yield curve, the chart plotting interest rates for different periods of time, should show a rise in rates as the term of debt lengthen.) Winter wheat, for instance, planted in the late fall and harvested in the late spring, would need to be shipped to an elevator and stored for a time before it theoretically could be delivered under a July, September, December contract or for the following year's March or May contracts—theoretically, that is, since almost no physical commodities are ever actually delivered to satisfy a contract. In contrast, what traders call a "backwardation," when the spot price exceeds futures or near month future exceeds distant months, is rarer; this can emerge when, for instance, news of an unexpected decline in supply or surge in demand or expectation of a usual seasonable variation is in the market. A modest backwardation had long been considered normal in the November shell egg future because of the historical pattern of a dip in egg shipments that month due to the biological fact that the pullets bought in the winter and early spring were aging and producing less. Exploiting a backwardation, with its implicitly less volatile risk premium was how the economist John Maynard Keynes had speculated, and with great success, too.[6]

Finally, the third test was that although Henner had staked out his basic position on the November contract, acting on his view that it would eventually hit 58 cents a dozen, he had not bothered to hit any of the offers earlier on June 25, when they ranged between 39.65 and 40.30 cents. Those offers were between 20 basis points below to 45 basis points above the close the day before, June 24. On that day, in fact, Henner could also have bought his nine contracts for even less.[7] The jump to 41.85 cents flouted a basic test of a real price, in Campbell's view—that buyers always tried for the lowest price they could secure and sellers for the highest. That Henner had not, and that he passed up earlier opportunities to buy futures at a lower price but moved only at the last second showed, for Campbell, a clear intention to set a fake price. Timing—when Henner acted and when he did not—was the critical, and novel, test in Campbell's analysis.

Beyond his three tests, Henner's actions showed an intention to manipulate the market, Campbell held. These were several. The first, that Henner bought only four November futures on June 24, the day before his buy the board and 41.85 cent deal, when the prices were much lower than 41.85 cents. The second, that he bought those four contracts right at the close of trading, as he had on June 25. The third, that since the closing price is the most significant price followed by futures traders, Henner waited until last few seconds of trading on June 25 to buy nine November futures instead of buying any of the sold earlier in the day between 39.65 cents and 40.30 cents. The fourth, that after buying the board at mostly higher prices, Henner then bid for one last contract at a still higher, limit up price of 41.85 cents a dozen. The fifth, that the 41.85 cents bid was 1.65 cents higher than Henner had just paid for the cheapest contract on egg futures ring blackboard (40.20 cents) and 55 points higher than the most expensive contract that the respondent had just purchased (41.30 cents). The sixth, that Henner did not ordinarily place bids for futures contracts. The seventh, that Henner's claim he bid limit up for just one last contract to round up a long position was contradicted by his transfer of the three most expensive contracts to Hoekstra after the close of trading on June 25, without replacing these even at the much lower prices available on June 26 or June 27. The eighth, that Henner acted when there was no new news about demand and supply in the late autumn. The ninth, that while the usual range of prices in the final minute of trading was not more than 0.2 cents, Henner's mark-up when buying the board and his final bid was a much larger: 1.65 cents with the 41.85 cent bid.[8]

Campbell's point here was that there was nothing except Henner's intention to account for a dramatic move in the price of the November future. The only news in the market on that day was Henner's trading in those final seconds. When the market settled down in the days that followed, the November future price remained more than one cent a dozen below Henner's limit up 41.85 cents; it remained at around that level through the summer.[9] "It is quite clear, and the inference is inescapable, that he increased his long position by intentionally trading in a manner that would raise the closing price of the November shell egg future on June 25 the full two cents permitted by the Exchange rules," Campbell concluded. Henner, he added, "intentionally paid more than he would have had to pay for November shell egg futures in order to cause the closing price on the Exchange to be two cents more than the previous day's settlement price. The respondent succeeded in creating an artificially high closing price for November shell egg futures."[10]

Henner, moreover, set the stage for this by waiting until just before the trading session was to end by buying the board, the move that, in addition to keeping Hoekstra from filling his stop loss orders, ensured that nobody else could make a bid for less than the limit-up 41.85 cents Henner called out right at the closing bell. After Marlowe King struck his deal, as Irving Manaster headed off the Mercantile bemoaning that he had not thought quickly enough to hit Henner's bid and an angry John Hoekstra complained Henner had cut him off from filling his clients' orders, Kenneth B. McKay, executive vice president of the Exchange decided he had to step in. Seeing the last minute flurry in the shell egg futures ring, McKay decided to speak to Henner a few minutes after trading ended on June 25, telling him he thought the deals "might have been construed as market manipulation," though McKay was not himself sure of that.[11]

Was one bid really enough to move a market, after all? Walter V. Sweeney, an egg broker and member of the Exchange since 1919, told the Commodity Exchange Authority that David Henner's moves to buy the board and then call out a limit-up, 41.85 cent bid was not a manipulation since "you can't manipulate the market with 10 contracts; you must have at least 500 contracts." Yet, when asked if a person could manipulate a futures price by buying it right at the close at the right price, he said "It could happen, but I really don't like the word 'manipulate.' I have never been in any kind of a deal like that."[12] Still, the sense that something was not right hung in the air. Henner had been bulling the market, as Arthur Parz would conclude, even though bulling, or forcing a price higher, typically involved making progressively higher bids sequentially, not all at once, by buying the board. Blackboard trades were supposed to involving matching posted offer with posted bid, one by one if there were more than one offer or one bid on the board. On June 25, there were no matching bids; nobody was buying. Until Henner, suddenly and at the last minute, was.

Traders might shrug their shoulders, but for a regulator like Campbell when trading—whether bulling the market or making a last minute, limit up bid far higher than the transactions immediately before—produced an artificial price it undermined the fundamental purpose of the market: price discovery for buyers and sellers of real eggs, a way of ensuring that farmers and shoppers alike got a fair deal. In his view, that was why the law banned manipulation and why it was his turn to enforce that law.[13] Others were not so sure. After Henner and King completed their deal, Kenneth McKay, the exchange's executive vice president told Henner he thought it looked like a manipulation, but he was not sure himself. Months later, the Exchange's directors would say only that Henner had impaired the dignity of the market. "I would say it was an atrocious purchase," said the economist L. Dee Belveal, testifying for Henner before a Commodity Exchange Authority hearing examiner. Yet just a few minutes later he also said that he believed that Henner had grounds for thinking the futures price would rise; "the case for price movement had preexisted the 25th of June for a good long time in terms of its fundamentals."[14] Then, asked during a later hearing before Judicial Offer Campbell if there had been any news that would have accounted for the sharp rise in price Henner's bid at the close had created, Belveal was clear: "There certainly was," he testified. "And without intending to be facetious, it was the only kind of news the market will listen to; namely, the news was that somebody wanted to buy the board and bid 41.85 for a bunch of contracts. This is the only communications the market understands."[15]

With this in mind, Campbell argued that Henner's last second deal was "perfectly timed to have an impact on the chartists."[16] Timing mattered, Campbell concluded, for when Henner "bid 41.85 at the ringing of the bell on June 25, it was not because he was so eager to have nine contracts instead of eight" as he later said was his motivation. "A strong inference is drawn from the fact that [Henner] claims that he was so eager for one more contract on June 25 that he bid the limit up, and then after giving away three contracts, he did not replace any of the three at much lower prices on June 26 or June 27," Campbell wrote. That inference: that Henner's moves were intended "to establish the closing quotation to be circulated throughout the country for that date at 41.85 cents," Campbell concluded.

By being absent from the shell egg pit and looking only at the condensed wisdom of the price, supposedly embodying (as economists might argue) all of the information available to producers, consumers and the various middlemen involved in bringing eggs from farm to grocery store, those speculators would not have seen the pace and pattern of trading. They would have had no chance at all to catch that easy to miss instant "when one trader comes on the floor with a deck of cards representing a substantial volume of purchases or sales he is about to make" and with "a mere wink of the eye, a tug at an ear, scratching the back of his head" could signal a friend on the other side of the pit "all that would be necessary for that trader to know he should buy or sell." In short, that moment when, as U.S. Representative Neal Smith, a Democrat from a corn belt district in central Iowa would later note "Tens of thousands of dollars can be made and artificial supply and demand provided."[17]

In the shell egg pit on June 25, then, an outsider seeking to divine egg market trends by looking at a price report would have missed the confusion, the angry complaint from Hoekstra that Henner had raided the market and Henner's transfer of his 41.85 cent deal and two others that should have made the point that these were not real purchases, even of notional eggs. None of that could have been spotted in the line in a newspaper or wire service market reports on the egg market. None of the small speculators Henner hoped would telephone their buy orders to brokerage firm branch offices would have heard anything about it. The message in the June 25 closing price for the November future was incomplete—but faith in the market meant that would not matter. "Those who follow charts exclusively, or to some extent, are legion! They can 'move' a market," as Belveal had written.[18]

By focusing on moving the daily closing price in the last seconds of the day's session, timing his moves so that nobody else could step in with a lower bid, Henner was aiming to signal a rally to speculators who were not in the pit—something the confused reaction to his 41.85 cent bid showed he could not have suggested to the other traders in the pit, who would have been looking for much more energetic trading involving at least a few more other traders before jumping on a bandwagon to push prices higher. One current handbook noted, "Many technicians use only the closing price as an indicator of the day's action."[19] On the other hand, some chart-watchers would plot bars, showing daily opening, high, low and closing prices and peer at the patterns these suggest in order to discern where prices will go next. In any event, all these speculators "insist that by analyzing *past* patterns traced out on a simple bar-chart, showing only daily (or weekly) trading ranges and closes, they can reliably project *future* price behavior," as Belveal wrote.[20]

This view of markets and prices suggested that for some chart-watchers, as opposed to many floor brokers who had seen the confusion following Henner's moves, the 41.85 cent closing price on June 25 confirmed that shell egg futures were about to rally. When looking for signs of where prices in financial markets will head, "Perhaps the most rudimentary of these is the simple relationship between price and volume," an early handbook on chart-based speculation advised. "If the price of a stock advances on increased volume of transactions (number of shares traded), this is regarded as 'bullish'—indicative that it will continue to advance."[21]

Tracking prices, such speculators would have seen a market that had seemed to have turned the day before, on June 24. A limit-up close—that 41.85 cent price that was the highest that Mercantile Exchange rules allowed for a single day's trading—looked like what basic handbooks for chart-watching called a penetration of resistance points. A resistance point, the theory goes, is established when prices rise to the same point two or more times and then back off. The theory behind this is that traders who had been willing to sell at the resistance point price had run out of securities or contracts to sell, or that some new information had changed their view about selling.[22]

Sometimes, to try to see more clearly through the fog of bouncing intra-day price variation—the random changes that the economist Paul Samuelson said were "more or less indistinguishable from white noise,"[23]—a chart-watcher with a more sophisticated approach than simply glancing at the close price might draw lines through a series of daily highs noted on a chart and another on the daily lows. Then, after extending the lines until they converged, the technical analysts would watch to see when prices might move either above or below the triangle formed by these supposed trend lines. These triangles were called bear flags or bull flags. A closing price that falls outside the line price is the chart-watcher's penetration of a resistance point. Double or triple tops or bottoms—lines that show a progression of daily prices touching and retreating from a high or low—were another signal that hopeful eyes might spot in charts, while "head and shoulders" is a triple top with the highest top coming in the middle of three and for some a strong signal that a rally was ending.[24] Henner's last second trades in the shell egg future on June 25 was intended to signal a resistance point breakthrough: a trade above the roughly 40.50 to 41 cent a dozen range where the November future had seemed stuck. It ended up being the central peak of an apparent head and shoulders pattern, at least as some chart-watchers might have seen it.

But except for Henner's extraordinary, apparently carefully timed limit up 41.85 cent bid, charting prices had a different message for Judicial Officer Campbell. The news from the market on June 25, up to the moment when Henner stepped forward to call out that he would buy the board was that what had been looking like a price rally had petered out, Campbell believed. The last completed trade before that more than forty-minute stretch when no buyer was interested in any of that wide range of offers would have looked more like it confirmed a resistance point: traders had backed off the 40-cent level for the November future, leaving the market on June 24 to close at 39.25 cents. By creating a limit-up close on June 25, cutting off any other possibility by buying the board just seconds before his 41.85 cent bid, Henner had simulated a penetration, or what Belveal's own manual on chart analysis for commodity markets called a "key reversal," Campbell argued.[25]

What was this? "In a nutshell, this is a trading session in which the last contingent of die-hard losers come to see the hopelessness of their situation," as Belveal described (and Campbell quoted) what a key reversal indicated. "Something happens to sink their last vestige of hope … Price soars, or plunges to a new contract high or low," he wrote. There is sudden pause, the scalpers—speculators who take out and unwind positions in a single session—begin taking their profits (or limiting their losses) and as volume begins to rise "price is now headed in the opposite direction from that of a few minutes ago." In a real reversal, as happened with Henner's well-timed move, "the closing price for the session will be significantly higher or lower than the preceding day's close."[26]

Moreover, Campbell continued, chartists who plot so-called "oscillators" might also have been misled by Henner's moves on June 25, since these technical indicators were based on the measurement of the price change rather than the price level. Looking at change rather than level signals an impending reversal, as one trading handbook that Campbell quoted had detailed in advising the use of these price signals.[27] Ultimately, the drama of a big move up might have been sufficient, whether or not a peering at a chart revealed a key reversal or oscillator, Campbell concluded cited that same handbook's view that traders aim to "buy strength and sell weakness" believing that such strength or weakness tends to continue.[28] In the end, while traders will take different—often sharply different—views on whether a market price at any one moment is correct, since some sell expecting prices to fall, and others buy in hopes of a price rise, "Some traders have much confidence in their judgment of the situation; others, very little," the handbook's authors noted. For the confident, when considering a chance in their stance, or the less certain "the slightest factor is likely to push them over the line."[29]

If Henner's last, limit-up deal looked like a real price to speculators across the country—traders who were not actually in the shell egg pit—he would have been able to spark enough interest by brokerage houses, commodity newsletter writers, traders, etc., to cause a sustained price advance, Judicial Officer Campbell wrote,[30] before once again quoting Belveal that "'Price ... for the market technician, we submit that its greatest significance is in the 'domino effect' it triggers in the course of its fluctuations.'"[31]

For such a signal to work, however, the chart-watcher tracking prices from an actively traded open outcry market, like egg futures market, assumes a large number of traders each of whom is free to contract with the others and then to strike new deals that cancel earlier transactions: perfect competition that perfectly determines a real price, while anything less (as the economist Francis Ysidro Edgeworth will point out in the next chapter) means a more or less indeterminate result—exactly what the message from the shell egg futures pit was on June 25.[32]

Often, in tales of markets, as in the charts of a technical analysts, prices are the result of dispassionate interaction of purely rational individuals—or, as the mathematics of markets we are about to explore, the even more ethereal interactions of aggregates of ... individuals? Firms? Yet if so, asked the economist Aaron Johnson, testing a theory—widely held by farmers—that futures trading in onions had distorted prices in the years before that before that market would be outlawed, why do models of The Market assume so much about them? Those assumptions include competition between buyers and among sellers, as well as between buyer and seller; perfectly divisible product, essentially equal access to information about supply and demand. "Economists have been so enamored with the perfectly competitive market that they have failed to raise the relevant question concerning the process whereby price is actually determined in the marketplace," he wrote.[33] Discovering an equilibrium between demand and supply may be a dynamic process, but once price is discovered and equilibrium established, why would it move?

Between noon and 12:45 p.m. on June 25, there was no change in the factors that could affect the supply of eggs or demand of eggs in November that could have reached the floor of the Chicago Mercantile Exchange: no word of farmers culling older hens or bringing in more pullets, no word of people jotting down shopping lists for Thanksgiving baking. No such word, in fact, for the next twenty hours, when trading resumed on June 26, with the November future immediately falling to 40.50 cents. The only change in supply was Henner's creation of that one, last November future; it was futures contracts, not eggs, that the shell egg futures pit brokers were trading, after all.

"Do I need a crystal ball to tell me price will rise enough for it to pay me to store corn today? No." wrote the economist Paul Samuelson in a textbook that introduced mainstream economic theory to hundreds of thousands of university students from the 1950s on—many of whom would become the small time speculators who drove up trading volume on commodity exchanges and fueled the bull market in shares of stock of the 1950s and 1960s. "The market today will quote me a future price—for delivery of wheat some months from now—and when this future price sufficiently exceeds the current spot price for physical corn, I get the signal to store."[34] In 1965, for instance, Samuelson demonstrated (mathematically, that is) that properly anticipated futures prices fluctuate randomly, constituting the kind of martingale sequence that, in gambling, indicates a fair deal and that in futures markets, signals an accurate measure of that deal's crystallization of demand and supply calculations.[35] Samuelson went on from this to conclude that an examination of share prices, when properly adjusted for expected dividend payments (the return that buyers of shares were presumably seeking) changes in stock prices "are more or less indistinguishable from white noise."[36] Efficient markets spit out prices that vary randomly—but although he himself believed commodity and stock markets, along with other competitive markets where many buyers and sellers interact were efficient, he did note that seeing a random walk pattern is not proof a market is efficient.

Henner, arguing that finding he had manipulated the shell egg market said (through his attorney) that the "real issue is whether it is a proper policy for the law to require all traders to be chartists or technical traders, which in turn renders suspect and illegal all 'random walk' traders or transactions."[37] Despite Judicial Officer Campbell's belief that Henner was trying to generate a chart that would inspire technicians to bid up the price of the November future, Henner argued that he was simply a believer in the efficient market and that his trades were just the random walk variations that proved the market was efficient—and, therefore, not manipulated.

Henner had argued that in the Commodity Exchange Authority's allegation he had manipulated the shell egg price "real issue is whether it is a proper policy for the law to require all traders to be chartists or technical traders, which in turn renders suspect and illegal all 'random walk' traders or transactions." He added that if the Authority found he had manipulated the market, traders in futures market would be "compelled to point to specific and objective new information to justify his bidding a market the limit up or down, or to justify objectively why he is taking the short side of a predominantly bullish market" or to be "responsible for the action or reaction time of fellow traders, or the refusal of traders to similarly and simultaneously interpret the worth of a November egg contract." He added that any price changes larger than a 5/100ths of a cent move in egg futures trading would be read as a market manipulation. Judicial Officer Campbell said that was a ridiculous claim. "The law does not require all traders to be chartists, or technical traders," Campbell wrote, adding:

> A trader is entitled to hear, in the words of Thoreau, a 'different drummer,' and to 'step to the music which he hears.' But he cannot force the drummer to play his tune. This is what the respondent did. He was not satisfied with the price determined by the free forces of supply and demand on the Exchange, so he intentionally distorted the price. This he must not do.[38]

In the end, if Henner was trying to spark a rally, he failed, as the Commodity Exchange Authority hearing examiner's initial review of the manipulation charge noted. "A free market, operating on the basis of the law of supply and demand, is, in effect, self-policing or self-correcting with respect to prices," the hearing examiner wrote. "While it is conceivable that persistent and continuous bidding up of the price of a commodity over an extended period of time by itself, with no other influences at work, could result in manipulation of prices ... The effect of respondent's trades was effectively and promptly negated in the free market by the very next trade on June 26."[39]

One reason why was almost certainly that it involved only one contract; and, moreover, one that other traders in the shell egg pit would have seen was unreal because Henner immediately transferred it and the two highest priced contracts he had seconds earlier acquired when he bought to board to John Hoekstra, to quieten his complaint that Henner had raided the market. How could that last contract be the real price, Campbell and traders in the shell egg futures pit asked, if Henner did not want to keep what he had bought? Within the tight, intimate and knowing circle of the shell egg futures pit, Henner's bid for just one contract, even buying the board, could not simulate the kind of market Edgeworth described and that was what chart-watchers necessarily had to believe in. The other traders knew better. For all the confusion and Hoekstra's anger about Henner's buying the board and then making that bizarre two-cent limit up, the other traders knew there had been no real break from the consensus that the future was worth somewhere around 39 to 40 cents.

What was the trend just before the closing bell, the traders might have wondered: was Henner buying the board up from 40.20 cents to 41.30 cents, or down, from 41.30 to 40.20 cents: bulling a market or trying to push it down? When Marlowe King hit Henner's final 41.85 cent bid as the last echo of the closing bell faded, cutting off any possible trade, like floor broker Raymond Elster's purchase of a November future at 40.50 cents at the opening bell on June 26, after seeing that the bids and offers called out showed a market that "was back in line." For Elster, it was not that 41.85 cents was out of line with where fresh eggs might have sold in but that the price of the November future was out of line with prices of the October and December futures.[40]

For Belveal, it did not matter that Henner's bid might have seemed out of line. It complied with Mercantile Exchange rules and it was not a big enough price change and did not give him enough November contracts to enable him to dictate prices going forward to be a manipulation. "In the absence of some evidence of intent, opportunity to profit, device, design, collusion, or whatever, I can't look at a chart and tell you whether it was manipulative or not. And I really fail to see how anybody could," he testified.[41] The "sheer force of orders ... reflected in some body saying 'I'll buy the board and I'll buy another contract'" might move a price but it would not be a manipulated, unreal price, Belveal said, since "I can't conceive of manipulation without intent. I can't conceive of manipulation being on a split-second basis."[42]

If Henner's trades on the closing bell on June 25 were deemed a manipulation, Belveal continued, "then I would certainly hate to be the unfortunate soul that buys the high price on a price reversal, or the low price on a price reversal ... the possibility is inherent in my bad judgment to also open me to the question of having manipulated the market." At this early stage of the investigation, the sympathetic hearing examiner who would eventually conclude Henner had not manipulated the market was moved to muse: "In being wrong, is that manipulation?" Belveal quickly picked up the cue. "Fifty percent of the people who are holding positions in the market are always wrong, because you can't have an open position without having a short on one side and a long on the other side," Belveal replied. "Now, being aware, sir, that David Henner bought the board in the last minute of trading and bid it up to 41.85 within the time permitted afterwards, given your knowledge and experience in the market, is that a manipulation or an attempted manipulation in your judgment?" the hearing examiner asked. "I can't tell you what was in the mind of a trader in the market. They burned the witches in Salem who [did] that, and I am not going to try to do that," Belveal said.[43]

NOTES

1. Henner's position before June 25, 1968 (from In re Henner, 1166–1167).

Contracts	Price
28	37.85
5	39.3
3	39.25
7	39.95
6	40.9
4	39.9
2	40.5
3	39.75
1	40
Total	Average
59	38.97

2. Ibid., 1180.
3. In re Henner, 1169.
4. Ibid., 1171–1172.
5. Ibid., 1171, 1173.
6. In June 1937, for instance, Keynes had a long position of 11 July wheat futures (each for notional delivery in Liverpool of 480,000 pounds of wheat, presumably from Canada) for which he had theoretically promised to buy for 8 shillings, 8–17/32nds pence a hundredweight. The spot price for wheat in early June was 8 shillings 11–5/8 pence per hundredweight. As the future began converging on the spot price, Keynes unwound four contracts in June with four shorts, taking a profit of £704; he did the same by with five more by mid-July, for an additional £1,320 profit. He cashed in the other three contracts, too, but used the proceeds to go long in October and December futures on the assumption that the high prices then prevailing for spot wheat (and on distant month Winnipeg and Chicago futures) would mean a continuing backwardation in Liverpool. Luca Fantacci, Maria Cristina Marcuzzo and Eleonora Sanfilippo, "Speculation in Commodities: Keynes' 'Practical Acquaintance with Futures Markets," *Journal of the History of Economic Thought*, Vol. 32, No. 3 (September 2010), 412–413.
7. In re Henner, 1189.
8. Ibid., 1221–1222.
9. Ibid., 1170–1171.
10. Ibid., 1174.
11. Ibid.,1255.
12. In re Henner, 1254.
13. Ibid., 1241.
14. Ibid., 1177, 1191.
15. Ibid., 1200, 1215.
16. Ibid., 1178.
17. *Review of Commodity Exchange Act and Discussion of Possible Changes: Hearings Before the House Comm. on Agriculture, 93d Cong., 1st Sess.* (Washington: Government Printing Office, 1973), 9–10.
18. Belveal, *Commodity Speculation with Profits in Mind* (Wilmette, Illinois: Commodities Press, 1967), 123.

19. Richard J. Teweles, Charles V. Harlow, and Herbert L. Stone, *The Commodity Futures Trading Guide* (New York: McGraw-Hill, 1969), 93.
20. Belveal, *Charting Commodity Price Behavior*, 49.
21. William P. Sargeant, *Stock Market Behavior; A Descriptive Guidebook for the New Investor* (New York: Exposition Press, 1957), 21.
22. Sargeant, *Stock Market Behavior*, 22.
23. Paul Samuelson, "Proof That Properly Discounted Present Values of Assets Vibrate Randomly." *The Bell Journal of Economics and Management Science*, Vol. 4, No. 2 (Autumn 1973), 369.
24. Sargeant, *Stock Market Behavior*, 24–26.
25. In re Henner, 1178.
26. Belveal, *Charting Commodity Market Price Behavior*, 122.
27. Teweles, Harlow, and Stone, *The Commodity Futures Trading Guide*, 99; oscillators and their analysis are described in more detail, Ibid., 99–107.
28. Ibid., 122–123.
29. In re Henner: 1178 quoting Frederick Thomsen, *Agricultural Prices* (New York: McGraw-Hill, 1952), 152.
30. Ibid., 1177.
31. Ibid., 1202, citing Belveal, *Charting Commodity Market Price Behavior*, 233.
32. Francis Ysidro Edgeworth, *Mathematical Psychics, an Essay on the Application of Mathematics to the Moral Sciences* (London: C Kegan Paul & Co, 1881), 20.
33. Aaron Johnson, *Effects of Futures Trading on Price Performance in the Cash Onion Market, 1930–1968*, U.S. Department of Agriculture Technical Bulletin 1470 (Washington: Government Printing Office, 1973), 12.
34. Paul Samuelson *Economics* (New York: McGraw Hill, 1973 [1948]), 421.
35. Paul Samuelson, "Proof That Properly Anticipated Prices Fluctuate Randomly" *Industrial Management Review*, Vol. 6, No. 2 (Spring 1965), 41–49.
36. Paul Samuelson, "Proof That Properly Discounted Present Values of Assets Vibrate Randomly." *The Bell Journal of Economics and Management Science*, Vol. 4, No. 2 (Autumn 1973), 369.
37. In re Henner, 1253.

38. Ibid.
39. Ibid., 1153–1154.
40. Ibid., 1215–1216.
41. Ibid., 1250.
42. Ibid., 1250.
43. Ibid., 1250, 1251.

REFERENCES

In re David G Henner, 30 Agricultural Decisions 1151

Review of Commodity Exchange Act and Discussion of Possible Changes: Hearings Before the House Comm. on Agriculture, 93d Cong., 1st Sess. (Washington: Government Printing Office, 1973)

Belveal, L. Dee: *Commodity Speculation with Profits in Mind* (Wilmette, Illinois: Commodities Press, 1967)

Economics (New York: McGraw Hill, 1973 [1948])

Edgeworth, Francis Ysidro: *Mathematical Psychics, an essay on the application of mathematics to the moral sciences* (London: C Kegan Paul & Co, 1881)

Fantacci, Luca, Maria Cristina Marcuzzo and Eleonora Sanfilippo: "Speculation in Commodities: Keynes' "Practical Acquaintance" with Futures Markets," *Journal of the History of Economic Thought*, Vol. 32, No. 3 (September 2010), 397–418

Johnson, Aaron: *Effects of Futures Trading on Price Performance in the Cash Onion Market, 1930–1968*, U.S. Department of Agriculture Technical Bulletin 1470 (Washington: Government Printing Office, 1973)

"Proof That Properly Anticipated Prices Fluctuate Randomly" *Industrial Management Review*, Vol. 6, No. 2 (Spring 1965), 41–49

Samuelson, Paul: "Proof That Properly Discounted Present Values of Assets Vibrate Randomly." *The Bell Journal of Economics and Management Science*, Vol. 4, No. 2 (Autumn 1973), 369–374

Sargeant, William: *Stock Market Behavior; a Descriptive Guidebook for the New Investor* (New York: Exposition Press, 1957)

Teweles, Richard J., Charles V. Harlow, and Herbert L. Stone: *The Commodity Futures Trading Guide* (New York: McGraw-Hill, 1969)

CHAPTER 4

Higgling

Abstract The first political economists seeking to explain how markets determined prices modeled barter markets in which actors were much like Henner and the other traders in the shell egg futures ring: where a trader might be both buying and selling at the same time—buying wheat and selling wine, in these first models, or bidding for eggs in the future by offering a contract, as in Henner's case. This renders ineffective the test that true prices result when buyers seek low prices and sellers, high ones. These early models, too, did not clear markets. Adam Smith, meanwhile, argued that market prices were not always the natural price that reflected the theoretical value of goods. Neoclassical theorists aimed to resolve this by proposing depersonalized, mathematically perfect market.

Keywords Futures · Bartering · Price theory · Markets

Some of the earliest writers exploring markets and prices started by placing themselves in spots much like standing alongside David Henner and Marlowe King in the Mercantile Exchange egg futures pit. Just as it is possible to ask if Henner had been bidding for eggs or offering a long futures contract, when in the eighteenth century Cesare Beccaria or Anne-Robert-Jacques Turgot tried to model a market by imagining exchanges between a wheat farmer and a wine maker, sorting out the buy side and

© The Author(s), under exclusive license to Springer Nature   49
Switzerland AG 2025
D. Ress, *Market Manipulation and The Price of Eggs*,
https://doi.org/10.1007/978-3-031-87171-9_4

the sell side of a market was not necessarily straightforward. Henner, in bidding 41.85 cents for eggs supposedly (but not actually) to be delivered in November, was actually trying to sell a contract, a notional promise to buy that neither he nor his counter-party, Marlowe King, ever expected to execute. To explain markets, Beccaria and Turgot (perhaps the first writers to venture into price theory since John Duns Scotus wrote that a bit of give and take produced a just price[1]) looked at bartering one good for another: wine for wheat. The problem with this can take a moment or two to see. How do you ask who has come to this market seeking to buy low and who has come seeking to sell high, Judicial Officer Donald Campbell's test for honest price determination. Was the farmer selling wheat or buying wine or was the vintner buying wheat or selling wine?

In the same way it may not be all that clear whether, on that June 25 afternoon, Henner was trying to buy eggs at a high price—an artificial, false price, that is—or if he had been selling a contract for eggs at a high price in a perfectly rational manner. If the actors in a market can simultaneously be both buyer and seller, as when bartering, where do you look to see that market striking its balance between demand and supply? Who is supplying? Who demanding?

By the time Beccaria and Turgot first explored the dynamics of a market, most exchanges involved an obvious seller—the person or store or company with goods on hand or services on offer—and an obvious buyer: the person with money (cash or credit) and a need or desire for the goods or services in question. Yet both Beccaria and Turgot looked at what they felt were the most basic exchanges of all, the bartering of goods, in order to propose a general theory of prices that would demonstrate that the free exchange of goods would ensure the correct valuation of those goods. Beccaria, whose treatise *Die Delitti e Del Penne* (Of Crimes and Punishments) was an early condemnation of the death penalty, was expanding on the notions from ancient Greece and from medieval church fathers that questions about prices and the value of goods were essentially questions about justice. Turgot, a provincial agent of the king of France who would eventually rise to service as Louis XVI's Controller General of Finance, was concerned with the sources of revenue for the crown.

That there could be a single, true price had long seemed self-evident. In what may well be the first written market report, Herodotus, in the fifth century BCE reported that when the traders of Carthage ventured beyond the Pillars of Hercules, they would lay out their various goods on the beach, and then, returning to their ships, light a large, smoky fire to signal that they were ready to barter: their textiles and manufactures for the gold that the peoples of the interior had panned from alluvial deposits on the upper Niger and Faleme rivers. "The natives, when they see the smoke, come down to the shore, and, laying out to view so much gold as they think the worth of the wares, withdraw to a distance," Herodotus wrote. The Carthaginians then return to the beach and "If they think the gold enough, they take it and go their way; but if it does not seem to them sufficient, they go aboard ship once more and wait patiently" until the Africans add more gold. The Carthaginians never touch the gold until they feel it represents a fair exchange; the Africans do not carry away the goods they bartered for until the Carthaginians take their gold.[2] The result was satisfactory to both sides, or so Herodotus' Carthaginian sources apparently told him, as he never seems to have traveled to the West African shore where the trade took place. This market, after all, had cleared: all the goods and all the gold were exchanged. Still, that declaration of mutual satisfaction did come from the initiator of the trade, and from the party that had made the other side come back with a richer bid. The Carthaginians, like Henner with his 41.85 cent bid, had set the price.

In the context of a bartering of goods, the true price is an exchange of everything of one for everything of the other. The test of the real price is that the market clears. The Carthaginians did not take their textiles and metalwork back when the Africans did not put down enough gold. The Africans did not just walk away when it seemed as if the cost of those textiles and metal goods was too high. It would have been a long trip back to Carthage for the traders, after all, and it would be tiring to carry the gold back home from the beach. The option was never to take it or leave it; the market was biased toward completing a deal of some kind. Yet trade here was not the antagonistic confrontation of Belveal's eyeball to eyeball dealing or the battle that other economists we will shortly encounter saw when buyer and seller meet: what Herodotus described was more in the nature of conversation, albeit a wordless one, aimed at finding a deal that did justice to both parties.

Nevertheless, Beccaria had a hard time balancing supply and demand as he imagined wheat farmers who wanted wine and wine-makers who needed wheat. With one farmer who had twelve bags of wheat and a vintner with six barrels of wine, the exchange at a natural, market clearing price was simple: two bags of wheat for one barrel of wine. The ratio of wheat to wine brought to market was the value of each. Add one more farmer, and say one had seven bags and the other five, as Beccaria then did, and things got more complicated. For at two for one ratio to clear the market the larger farmer would get three barrels of wine but would be left with an unexchanged bag of wheat. If the smaller farmer got the remaining three barrels, the exchange ratio would dropped to one and two thirds bags of wheat for a barrel: the exchange price would fall from the natural price. If the wine-maker did not want to accept that and insisted on the two for one price, then the smaller farmer would get two-and-a-half barrels, and the wine-maker would be stuck with a half-a-barrel of unexchanged wine. "If need and market soundings are unequal," so that the larger farmer is thirstier for wine, the exchange price of wheat will fall, Beccaria wrote. "[T]he value of a thing generally decreases as the number of sellers increases," he added, but without noticing that the market had not cleared.[3]

Add yet another actor and imagine two farmers and two wine-makers bringing a total of sixteen bags of wheat and fifteen measures of wine to market, as Beccaria does next, and things get even more complex. To clear the market, exchanging all the wheat for all the wine, the market-clearing price of wheat (as Beccaria does not calculate) would be 0.9375 measures of wine (or, alternatively, the price of wine would be 1.0625 bags of wheat). But in this scenario, one farmer has twelve bags of wheat on offer, the other only four. On the other side of the market one wine-maker has six measures and the other, nine. What happens in this market, Beccaria argues, is that the exchange price of wheat will rise. Instead of the nearly one for one market clearing price, the smaller wine maker might try to buy at that price, but the larger winemaker can offer as much as 1.5 measures of wine for one measure of wheat. "Because the one who has only six measures of wine will always have to increase the offering price and the one with nine will always have to decrease it, this contrary motion will have to end when the offers meet at the same price."[4] In this case, then, Beccaria says the smaller vintner's offer increases from one to 1.25; the larger one's declines from 1.5 to 1.25. But Beccaria stops here, not noticing that at that 1.25 to one ratio, the wine-makers might have acquired all the wheat, but would still go home with 2.2 measures of wine unexchanged. The exchange price is not the ratio of the supply of wheat to the supply of wine, the price that would move all the wine.

It was by ignoring how much wheat and how much wine is available that Anne-Robert-Jacques Turgot, baron de l'Aulne, would consider bartering and say traders for whom "it is natural that each should wish to receive as much and give as little as he can" find the true price.[5] They will seek varying prices "according as one of them happens to have a more or less pressing need of the commodity belonging to the other."[6] One wheat farmer—much as Henner did when he was offering to sell a contract to buy eggs at 41.85 cents—might call out an offer price of one bushel for six pints of wine, another farmer might then offer eight and yet another, four, but "each has to balance the attachment he has for the commodity he gives against the desire he has for the commodity he wishes to receive."[7] The price, then, "is fixed by the balance of the wants and capabilities of all the sellers of wheat with those of all the sellers of wine." The wine-maker who would willing exchange eight pints of wine for a bushel of wheat will even more willingly pay only four when he learns that there is a wheat farmer who would exchange two bushels for eight pints, and in the end, "The price mid-way between the different offers and the different demands will become the current price."[8]

Turgot then asked what might happen when the quality of goods offered for exchange varies: Anjou wine versus wine from the Cape or a fat pullet instead of an aging fryer chicken. "If eighteen pints of wine of Anjou are equivalent in value to a sheep, eighteen pints of Cape wine could be equivalent to eighteen sheep," Turgot writes. That means that "he who to express the value of a sheep, would say it is worth eighteen pints of wine, would employ an equivocal language, and would not communicate any precise idea," he wrote. But "the cooks of Paris, and the fishmongers who furnish great houses," while thinking of a categorical value in terms of a abstract chicken or fish—a "piece"—were able to adjust for varying quality, for "A fat pullet is esteemed one piece, a chicken half a piece, more or less."[9]

Here, the various bids and offers settle around the mid-price for an abstract commodity: "wine" rather than "Anjou wine," "chicken" instead of a young hen versus a stringy old rooster. Price for the category—something rather like a November shell egg futures contract for a car lot of white, large Grade A eggs delivered at specified Chicago warehouses in the final week of November 1968 that Henner traded—is set by the market, in which the ratio of bartered goods any one individual is willing to accept is adjusted by what everyone else is willing to do. Any buyer's preference for a more tender chicken, or for a more refined wine, like any negotiation for, say, Farmer Jones's brown, medium eggs deliverable in Iowa or Smith's large white-shelled ones available in California, determine a premium or discount from that mid-point market price for the abstract commodity.[10] The willing buyer and seller, that is, are bargaining over a variation from the market price, the midpoint at which all buyers and sellers of all varieties of a commodity are willing to deal.

Here, however, Turgot is not describing bartering. Those cooks and fishmongers are not accepting other goods in exchange. Turgot is describing sales for money, for it was (and is) the introduction of money, the cowrie shells used in African and southeast Asian commerce, the apricot seeds scholars used for their gaming, or the copper coins the Romans struck, made possible the kind of precise communication of value that bartering Anjou or Cape wine for sheep could not.[11] Money changes the structure of a marketplace exchange: supply and demand are clearer: the individual with goods to sell is supply, the individual with money and with a desire or need for a good is demand. Moreover, because money is divisible in degrees that many bartered goods are not—a buyer can bid, say 41.85 cents a dozen for a standard lot of 600 cases of eggs in Chicago in November instead of 40.3 cents, for instance—it makes possible a critically important assumption of the ideal market of theory: infinitesimally divisible goods, innumerably and indeterminately large numbers of buyers and sellers.

What then is the real price of wheat and wine? The paths that Beccaria and Turgot followed, generalizing from their wheat farmers and vintners, leave the question open. At 1.25 measures of wine for a bag a wheat, there were still 2.2 measures of wine left unexchanged; Turgot's midpoint of six pints per bushel leaves the question of whether the market cleared unanswered since he does not say anything about supply; when he does, and it is a matter of a fat pullet or stringy fryer, the seller says the real value of what is on offer is a function of its quality compared to the categorical ideal—or so, in any event the real commerce of Parisian cooks suggests.

That the price agreed in a marketplace might not reflect the real value of a good troubled Adam Smith, writing a few years after Turgot. In his modeling of market exchange, which did not assume barter as a basic condition, Smith argued that the prices reached "by the higgling and bargaining of the market" approach but do not necessarily settle on what he called the "natural price" of goods or services. For Smith this was the sum that covered the costs of labor, capital and natural resources goods embodied; market prices were merely "sufficient for carrying on the business of common life."[12] Sufficient, perhaps, but the goods demanded at any particular time might not be sufficient to meet what Smith called "effectual demand": demand, that is, from buyers who could afford the natural price. In that case, the higgling of the marketplace would settle on an exchange price that would be artificially—that is, unnaturally—high. On the other hand, if effectual demand were insufficient, the exchange price would be artificially low, and new buyers who might not be able to afford the natural price would enter the market.[13]

For Smith, the natural price is a function of producers' costs and profit and a market price was almost inevitably an artificial one, unless a given supply was exactly as much as effectual demand. This effectual demand was also a given since "A very poor man" might want a fancy carriage and team of horses: "he might like to have it; but ... the commodity can never be brought to market" at a price he could afford, as Smith put it.[14] While higgling could not always balance aggregate demand with supply,[15] Smith said balance came with the post-higgling decisions of producers, when landlords "withdraw a part of their land" or "prepare more land for the raising of this commodity" or when workers and employers "withdraw a part of their labour or stock from this employment," or "employ more labour and stock."[16]

Despite Smith, higgling—bargaining over the price of goods—is at the heart of many stories about markets. It is, for example, the way markets are presented in a popular introductory economics textbook Henner's day. In this tale, Farmer Pratt when chatting to his neighbor, Farmer Judson, "lets fall the hint that he might be interested" in buying a wood lot. Judson "cagily replies that he had no thought of selling" but would listen to an offer "the business of bargaining commences." The conversation then starts with Pratt's bid of $200, which Judson dismisses, declaring that his wood lot is worth at least $750. The first replies that he could bid as much as $300; the second that he might ask as little as $675. The back and forth continues from there. If Pratt is very eager to get the wood lot, perhaps because he has a chance to sell some timber, and the second was not particularly interested in selling, higgling would resolve upon a high price; if the second farmer was more interested in selling, perhaps because he needed cash for other bills, the final price of any deal might be lower. Finally, if Pratt had in mind that the most he could bid was, say, $400, and the second firm in his feeling that he could not accept less than, for example that $675, there would be no sale.[17]

Farmers Pratt and Judson might find a price between the buyer's desired low and the seller's hoped for high by higgling—though this did not always end up satisfying both, as one popular 1960s writer of marketing advice detailed from a holiday in Mexico. The shopkeeper says the price for a cigarette lighter is thirty pesos; the writer, Elmer Wheeler, replies (in poor Spanish) that it is too much, and counters with a bid of twenty pesos. Twenty-seven, the shopkeeper suggests. "Divide!" a now firm Wheeler says, thinking he is driving a hard bargain by cutting his bid in half. They agree on that thirteen and a half peso price. Afterward, chided by a friend for not pressing harder for a steep price cut, Wheeler insisted he "obtained a Ronson lighter at a fair price." His friend suggested he check. When he did, he found the small print on the lighter's base said: Ransom.[18] Perhaps in that case, Wheeler did not say, he had successfully bargained for the true price for what he ended up buying?

"Higgling-haggling has been rightly recognized as being of the essence of bargaining behavior," the economist Karl Polanyi noted, but "exchange at fluctuating prices aims at a gain that can be attained only by an attitude involving ... the element of antagonism." There is a winner and loser, in short, and this fact "is ineradicable."[19] Yet if exchange is essential in holding human society together, the need for social peace tends to limit higgling, Polanyi argued. Tribal societies and feudal societies emphasize gift exchanges, whether through channels of kinship or fealty; states move toward administered prices to cut off the higgling with that inherent element of conflict, as with the dictated grain prices of ancient Athens and Rome—as well, for that matter, as the prices grocers post over their produce or a steelmaker publishes in a catalogue. With administered prices "higgling-haggling is no longer part of the proceedings; rather, the purpose is to exclude it." The market is simply the forum where buyers can take or leave a dictated price, a mechanism that resolves upon a price without the antagonism of higgling, Polanyi wrote. There is no aggrieved John Hoekstra in this kind of market, unlike the egg futures ring.[20]

From the assumption of higgling as the means of finding prices, it is not too large a leap to see the interaction of buyer and seller as a conflict. This battling "goes all the way back into the far mists of history when sales and purchases first were made," as Cornell University's Herrell F. DeGraff, a leading agricultural economist of 1940s to 1980s, told his students. "Fundamentally every transaction that you or I or anyone makes is the same kind of price battle that takes place in a grain pit," DeGraff wrote. Even "a housewife's grocery purchases in a supermarket" is battle, DeGraff continued. Each price tag and each time those shoppers "balancing their families' needs and the content of their purses against the

price tags" place an item in their carts, "demonstrates a fundamental principle of the marketplace ... No seller will take less than is necessary to
move his produce; no buyer will pay more than necessary to satisfy his
needs.[21]

If, on the other hand and despite Smith, it is higgling that balances
supply and demand, whether of a categorical product—a Mercantile
Exchange futures contract's set amount of eggs of a standard quality eggs
in a Chicago warehouses in the last week of November 1968—or Farmer
Jones' brown eggs, it is not obvious that there was any higgling in the
shell egg futures pit on June 25 1968. At the start of trading on the
morning of June 25, during the brief, five minute open outcry trading in
the shell egg futures pit, David Henner would have noted three contracts
traded at the previous day's close, a price 1/10th of a cent higher than
three contracts he himself had purchased that day but 15/100ths of a cent
below a later deal he also struck that day: the opening price was right at
the midpoint if Henner's June 24 transactions. Then, two minutes after
the June 25 opening bell, as open outcry wound down, two traders struck
one more deal, at 15/100ths of a cent below the first three: the market
was now down. As traders then posted bids and offers on the trading
pit blackboard, the first deal struck fell another 10/100ths. Then, over
the next 45 minutes, in five steps of 5/100ths to 20/100ths each, the
price rose to 40.20 cents, up at that point 35/100ths of a cent from the
previous day's close—tentatively headed, that is, in the direction Henner
wanted.

But after the longest pause of the day to that point, some twenty
minutes, the next trade came 15/100ths down; followed immediately by
another trade another 5/100ths down, giving up much but not yet all of
the gains so far that day. After another 25-minute pause, the next trade
came between these two, at 40.10 cents; then yet another 25-minute
pause before a tiny flurry of five trades, all at 40.20 cents, followed five
minutes later by two more, the first at 40.25 cents, the second back at
40.20 cents. After a half hour, two traders struck a deal at 40.30 cents, the
day's high. Over the next 40 minutes, traders chalked offers on the board
that ranged between 40.20 and 41.30 cents, at which point, with seconds
to go before the closing bell, Henner shouted out that he would buy
the board.[22] The back-and-forth Smith described (much as Herodotus
or Duns Scotus had) was not what Henner and Marlowe King did, nor
was it what buying the board a few seconds earlier entailed.

Nor had Henner higgled when buying the board. Buying the board meant accepting varying asking prices from varying offerors; though this happened simultaneously, it did not involve the dance of buyer and seller that in the metaphor of higgling, explained how both parties would complete an exchange that left them both satisfied. "Why should I be content with a promise to receive $7,236 in November, when the fellow next to me gets at the exact same time a promise for $7,434?" the trader who offered the 40.2 cent price on the shell egg pit blackboard might well have asked (but likely had not). Henner's "buy the board" move belies the notion that "the law of one price still truly prevails" on commodity exchanges, a point the economist G. Wright Hoffman wrote. helps demonstrate markets like the Chicago Mercantile Exchange were "probably the leading examples today of purely competitive markets."[23]

For in such a purely competitive market, Henner and the other brokers in in the shell egg futures pit at 12:45 p.m. on June 25 1968, were much like the individual Leon Walras hypothesized in sketching his mathematical model of markets' price determination: a "*porteur*" (holder) of wheat—someone, that is, who was not necessarily a producer or consumer. With Walras's somewhat subtle elision of the question of what gets produced and brought to market and who does that work, "if our man himself comes to the market," he could keep his notions about the prices where he would strike a deal to himself. These would be virtual, not effective prices until some else called out a bid and the *porteur* agreed. If the *porteur* did not come to the market in person (as John Hoekstra's clients had not), but simply handed notes to a friend or agent detailing various amount of wheat "from zero to infinity" he would be willing to exchange for various amounts of oats (or francs or dollars or wheat futures contracts) the result might be something rather like the blackboard in the shell egg pit. But it could also be drawn as a curve on a graph (with price on one axis and quantity on the other), essentially a demand curve for oats (or francs, or dollars or long egg futures) expressed in terms of wheat (or short futures).[24] Then, the machinery of the market in effect would add up all the same curves for all traders with wheat, all the corresponding curves for those with oats (or francs and so forth), and then superimpose them all. What pops up is the equilibrium price. As other actors in the market considered those offers it would be a simple matter of mathematics for the machinery of the market to settle on a price "We are now in a position to see clearly what the mechanism of market competition is," namely the real-world expression of the mathematics, Walras concluded.[25]

It was this mathematics, Walras continued, that yielded the most efficient allocation of resources for production—capital, labor and natural resources—as well as the fairest distribution of products, for embedded in the *porteur*'s lists of how much he would give for how much in return, as in the lists of all the other many actors in the market, were the points beyond which none of them would go, those points where the satisfaction gained by selling or buying one more item would begin to decline. When discovered by the mechanics of the market, all the actors were as well off as possible, and the price dictated what was produced, who would make it and get it and who would get what return.

One model of what would become the predominant way of thinking about the instantaneous way markets found true prices—and it actually was a model—was the twentieth century American economist Irving Fisher's. Fisher imagined (and later built), a kind of large rectangular basin, in which rows of linked and carefully shaped small containers floated. The small containers could express, like a three-dimensional graph of an equation, as an individual's demand for a given product to model the distribution of goods or equally a producer's marginal cost if considering the supply side of a market. Each row of small containers, then, represented any single consumer's demand for a range of products (or a producer's alternatives for what goods to offer), each column of small containers representing different consumers' differing demands (or various producers' different costs). Each small container held an amount of water representing the amount of goods purchased (and therefore produced); as water in the large basin rises or fall, each small container fills or empties at rates determined by its shape and finds a new point at which it is buoyant and price, quantity and distribution of goods or allocation among producers is determined. The mechanism is automatic; prices are universally known, and since the water level in the small containers matches the water level in the larger basin, prices are constant for the economy modeled. Everything made is consumed and even if individuals buy different amounts (or producers make different quantities), the price of each unit sold is the same. The model works smoothly and automatically to determine the real value of goods, both to the consumer and to the maker; the process arriving them is as easy and natural as a flow of water.[26] People—real traders, David Henners and Marlowe Kings and Irving Manasters and John Hoekstras are absent, even if they were clearly present in the free market of the shell egg futures pit.

In any event, Hoffman's law of one price can fail in a market, the nineteenth century English economist Francis Ysidro Edgeworth pointed out. The reason is that to be a willing buyer or willing seller means an intention to act with the consent of others affected by your actions; otherwise, price is dictated—take or leave it. "The first principle of economics is that every agent is actuated only by self-interest," held that the resolution of those self-interests comes "according as the agent acts *without*, or *with*, the consent of others affected by his actions"—through what he called war or contract.[27] Edgeworth's war was not DeGraff's metaphor of the battle in the supermarket or Belveal's eyeball to eyeball confrontation, but neither of those metaphors was anything close to Edgeworth's free, competitive market. For perfect competition, Edgeworth wrote, each actor needs to be free to contract with any number of others—and then to strike new deals with any number, deals that cancel the initial contract; striking those new deals do not require consent of the actors in the initial contract. A perfect, free market, then, might look something like the din of shouted bids and offers, the unending dance of hand gestures across a commodity exchange trading ring as buyers and sellers probe for where to strike their deals for millions of bushels of wheat or soybeans—or shell egg futures.

Still, "Contract with perfect competition is perfectly determinate ... Contract with more or less perfect competition is less or more indeterminate," Edgeworth wrote.[28] So then, at what point do just two individuals agree; David Henner and Marlowe King over a November futures contract, or Robinson Crusoe and Friday agree on what work Friday will do in exchange for what Crusoe will pay? The answer is anywhere along a curve, which Edgeworth called the contract curve, that represents a series of potential exchanges of varying sums paid for varying hours worked.[29]

The market here resolves not on a point—that one price of Hoffman's law of one price—that that tells us how many hours Friday will work and what Crusoe will but rather (expressed mathematically upon a curved line, a series of alternative quantities (in this case of hours worked) and prices (in this case, of wages). "This simple case," Edgeworth concludes, "brings clearly into view the characteristic evil of the indeterminate contract, deadlock, undecidable opposition of interest ... It is in the interest of both parties that there be some settlement ... But which of these contracts [that is, points along contract curve] is arbitrary." In short, "An accessory evil of indeterminate contract is the tendency, greater than in a full market, towards dissimulation and the objectionable arts of higgling."[30] "Proceeding by degrees from the case of two isolated bargainers to the limiting case of a perfect market, we see how *contract is more or less indeterminate as the field is less or more affected by the first imperfection, limitation of numbers.*"[31]

NOTES

1. John Duns Scotus, Questiones in IV librum sententiarum IV, 15, qu. 2 in *Opera omnia. Ed. nova juxta editionem Waddingi XII tomos continentem a patribus Franciscanis de observantia accurate recognita*, Vol. 18 (Paris: Apud L. Vivès, 1895), 283, 317, 318; Odd Langholm "Just Price," and "Scholastic Economics" in The New Palgrave Dictionary of Economics, https://doi.org/10.1057/978-1-349-95121-5_715-2 and https://doi.org/10.1057/978-1-349-95121-5_2755-1

2. Herodotus, *The History*, Book 4, Sect. 196 (the translation is in The History of Herodotus, George Rowlinson, tr. (New York, Tandy-Thomas, 1909), Vol. 2, 313–314.

3. Cesare Beccaria, *Elementi di economia pubblica* (Milan: G.G. Destafanis, 1804 [posthumous publication of lectures from1768–1770]), 346 "ma se i bisogni e le ricerche siano disuguali, cosicchè il posseditore delle 7 di fru mento abbia più bisogno di vino, il valore del frumento diminuirà: onde generalmente il va lore di una cosa diminuisce coll' accrescersi il numero de' venditori."

4. Ibid., 348. perchè quegli, che non ha che 6 misure di vino dovrà crescere sempre un poco l'esibizione, e quegli che ha le 9 dovrà sempre diminuirla: e questo moto contrario dovrà finire finchè il che non prezzo del s'incontrino al medesimo prezzo; può avvenire se non allora che il primo da 1 sarà asceso ad 1–1/4, e il prezzo del secondo disceso da 1–1-/2 ad 1-1/4.

5. Anne-Robert-Jacques Turgot, *Réflexions sur la formation et la distribution des richesses*, Reflection XXXI, paragraph 1 "Le besoin réciproque a introduit l'échange de ce qu'on avoit contre ce qu'on n'avoit pas ... dans cette convention il est naturel que chacun desire de recevoir le plus qu'il peut & de donner le moins qu'il peut...".

6. Ibid., "dans un autre échange entre d'autres hommes, ce prix sera différent, suivant que l'un d'eux aura un besoin plus ou moins pressant de la denrée de l'autre".

7. Ibid., "c'est à chacun d'eux à balancer l'attachement qu'il a pour la denrée qu'il donne avec le desir qu'il a de la denrée qu'il veut recevoir".

8. Ibid., La valeur du ble & du vin n'est plus débattue entre deux seuls Particuliers relativement à leurs besoins & à leurs facultés réciproques; elle se fixe par la balance des besoins & des facultés de la totalité des Vendeurs de ble avec ceux de la totalité des Vendeurs de vin. Car tel qui donneroit volontiers huit pintes de vin pour un boisseau de ble, n'en donnera que quatre lorsqu'il saura qu'un Propriétaire de ble consent à donner deux boisseaux de ble pour huit pintes. Le prix moyen entre les différentes offres & les différentes demandes deviendra le prix courant auquel tous les Acheteurs & les Vendeurs se conformeront dans leurs échanges; & il sera vrai de dire que six pintes de vin seront pour tout le monde l'équivalent d'un boisseau de bled, c'est- là le prix moyen, jusqu'à ce que la diminution de l'offre d'un côté, ou de la demande de l'autre, fasse changer cette évaluation.

9. Ibid., XXXVVI–XXXVII;. si dix-huit pintes de vin d'Anjou, sont l'équivalent d'un mouton, dix-huit pintes de vin du Cap seront l'équivalent de dix-huit moutons. Ainsi celui qui pour faire connoître la valeur d'un mouton, diroit qu'il vaut dix-huit pintes de vin, employeroit un langage équivoque, & qui ne donneroit aucune idée precise... un mouton, dans le langage du commerce, ne signifie qu'une certaine valeur, qui, dans l'esprit de ceux qui l'entendent, porte l'idée non-seulement d'un mouton, mais d'une certaine quantité de chacune des denrées les plus communes, qui font regardées comme l'équivalent de cette valeur; & cette expression finira si bien par s'appliquer à une valeur fictive & abstraite, plutôt qu'à un mouton reel.... Ainsi les rôtisseurs de Paris, les marchands de poisson, qui fournissent de grandes maisons, font ordinairement leurs marchés à la pièce. Une poularde grasse est comptée pour une pièce, un poulet pour une demi-pièce, plus ou moins....

10. Ibid.

11. Ibid., XLI.

12. Adam Smith, *An Inquiry into the Wealth of Nations*, Book I, chapter v, paragraph 4.

13. Ibid., I, vii, 8–9.

14. Ibid, I, v, 4; I vii, 8.

15. On a macro-economic scale, the twentieth century economist John Maynard Keynes would say this is the cause of recession or inflation; Keynes, *The General Theory of Employment, Interest and Money* (London: Macmillan, 1936).

16. Smith, *Wealth of Nations*, I, vii, 12–13.

17. Fred Rogers Fairchild, *Understanding Our Free Economy: An Introduction to Economics* (Princeton: Van Nostrand, 1956), 132–133.

18. Elmer Wheeler, *Around the World with Elmer ... Backwards; or, How to haggle in 17 countries* (New York: Fleet Publishing Corp., 1960), 27.

19. Karl Polanyi, "Semantics of General Economic History" (New York: Columbia University Research Project on Origins of Economic Institutions, 1953), 12.

20. Ibid., 16–17.

21. Herrell F. DeGraff, *Class Exercises, Agricultural Economics 159, Food Economics Spring Term 1961–1962* (Ithaca, N.Y.: New York State College of Agriculture, 1961), 91.

22. In re Henner, 1163–1164.

23. G. Wright Hoffman, *Futures Trading Upon Organized Commodity Markets in the United States* (Philadelphia: University of Pennsylvania Press, 1932), 251.

24. Leon Walras, *Éléments d'économie politique pure, ou, Théorie de la richesse sociale* (Lausanne:L. Corbaz,1874), 60: Si notre homme va lui-même sur le marché, il peut laisser ses dispositions à l'enchère à l'état virtuel et non effectif, c'est- à-dire ne déterminer sa demande de que le prix P_a une fois connu. Même alors ces dispositions n'en existent pas moins. Mais si, par exemple, il était empêché de se rendre en personne sur le marché, ou si, pour une raison ou pour une autre, il de- vait donner sa commission à un ami ou ses ordres à un agent, il devrait prévoir toutes les valeurs possibles de P_a, depuis zéro jusqu'à l'infini, et déterminer en conséquence toutes les valeurs correspondantes de da, en les exprimant d'une manière quelconque. Or toutes les personnes quelque peu habituées au calcul savent qu'il y a un double moyen de fournir cette expression mathématique.

25. Ibid., 69: On voit clairement à présent ce qu'est le mécanisme de la concurrence sur le marché: c'est la solution pratique. Walras' mathematical modeling of the market was very much a fashion

of his time in the late nineteenth century (and, indeed, of later economics thought). W. Stanley Jevons, for instance, in effect by flipping an analogue of one of the two curves Walras' geometric demonstration, made the same point about how a market (not the actors in a market) moves inexorably toward an equilibrium price at which everyone is satisfied and followed this with a proof in equations. "Strictly speaking, the ratio of exchange at any moment is that of dy to dx, of an infinitely small quantity of one commodity to the infinitely small quantity of another that is given for it" and there cannot be more than one price at any one instant. W. Stanley Jevons, *The Theory of Political Economy* (London: Macmillan and Co., 1879), 100–101, 106–108.

26. Irving Fisher, *Mathematical Investigations in the Theory of Value and Prices* (New Haven: Yale University Press, 1925[1892]), 24–52.

27. Francis Ysidro Edgeworth, *Mathematical Psychics, an Essay on the Application of Mathematics to the Moral Sciences* (London: C Kegan Paul & Co, 1881), 16–17.

28. Ibid., 20.

29. Ibid., 28–29.

30. Ibid., 29–30.

31. Ibid., 42. Emphasis in the original.

References

In re David G Henner, 30 Agricultural Decisions 1151

Beccaria, Cesare: *Elementi di economia pubblica* (Milan: G.G. Destafanis, 1804)

DeGraff, Herrell: *Class Exercises, Agricultural Economics 159, Food Economics Spring Term 1961–1962* (Ithaca, NY: New York State College of Agriculture, 1961)

Duns Scotus, John: Questiones in IV librum sententiarum IV, 15, qu. 2 in *Opera omnia. Ed. nova juxta editionem Waddingi XII tomos continentem a patribus Franciscanis de observantia accurate recognita*, Vol. 18 (Paris: Apud L. Vivès, 1895)

Edgeworth, Francis Ysidro: *Mathematical Psychics, an essay on the application of mathematics to the moral sciences* (London: C Kegan Paul & Co, 1881)

Fairchild, Fred Rogers: *Understanding Our Free Economy: An Introduction to Economics* (Princeton: Van Nostrand, 1956)

Fisher, Irving: *Mathematical Investigations in the Theory of Value and Prices* (New Haven: Yale University Press, 1925[1892])

Herodotus: *The History* (George Rowlinson, tr.) (New York, Tandy-Thomas, 1909)

Hoffman, G. Wright: *Futures Trading Upon Organized Commodity Markets in the United States* (Philadelphia: University of Pennsylvania Press, 1932)

Keynes, John Maynard: *The General Theory of Employment, Interest and Money* (London: Macmillan, 1936)

Polanyi, Karl: "Semantics of general economic history" (New York: Columbia University Research Project on Origins of Economic Institutions, 1953)

Smith, Adam: *An Inquiry into the Wealth of Nations* (New York: Cosimo Classics, 2007 [first published 1776])

Turgot, Anne-Robert-Jacques: *Réflexions sur la formation et la distribution des richesses* (New York: 1788 [first published 1770])

Walras, Leon: *Éléments d'économie politique pure, ou, Théorie de la richesse sociale* (Lausanne: L. Corbaz,1874)

Wheeler, Elmer: *Around the World with Elmer ... Backwards; or, How to Haggle in 17 Countries* (New York: Fleet Publishing Corp., 1960)

CHAPTER 5

The Human Factor

Abstract Markets, in theory, are about resolving individuals' varying views about the value of goods and services; dispassionate and impersonal interaction is the supposed process. David Henner argued that he had acted on this basis with his shell egg futures deals. Yet his gift of three of the contracts he acquired when he bought the board and made his final limit-up bid suggests dealings in a free wheeling open outcry market are not always dispassionate and impersonal, just as a look at the analysis underlying his mistakenly bullish stance might.

Keywords Markets · Prices · Futures contracts

In Daniel Dafoe's tale, as with the shell egg futures pit, it is not obvious that the market interactions between two individuals was really higgling: in Daniel Dafoe's story, after Robinson Crusoe rescued Friday, shared some bread, gave him clothing and took him hunting "I marked out a larger piece of land … in which Friday worked not only very willingly and very hard, but did it very cheerfully," the story goes. "He … let me know that he thought I had much more labour upon me on his account than I had for myself; and that he would work the harder for me if I would tell him what to do."[1] Higgling makes a good metaphor for the idea of negotiation in a market, but can be an uncomfortable one when

© The Author(s), under exclusive license to Springer Nature Switzerland AG 2025
D. Ress, *Market Manipulation and The Price of Eggs*,
https://doi.org/10.1007/978-3-031-87171-9_5

it comes to explaining a price because, as Edgeworth noted, it suggests the possibility of dishonest dealing. John Steinbeck's *Grapes of Wrath*, the novel that for many mid-century readers brought home the human cost of economic failure, described a used car deal that starts with the lot owner quoting $80 for a junker to a Dust Bowl farmer who says "I can't go no higher than fifty. The fella outside says fifty." The car dealer says he paid $78.50 for the car, but "might take $60" and maybe something in trade. How about my mules, the farmer offers. "Well I'm a sucker," the dealer says, and sells the car for the farmer's $50, as well as his promissory note for four monthly payments of $10 and the farmer's mules and wagon, which he later tells that "fella outside" he expects to sell for $75—and all for car, he adds, that he acquired for $30.[2] Higgling, the moral of this story concludes, does not always produce a real price—or at least honest dealing.

Dissimulation was a threat to futures markets, too, whether or not the actors or observers (or regulatory agency judicial officers) viewed open outcry dealing—I bid, you hit my bid; or you offer, I buy—as a kind of version of higgling or as an expression of Walras' or Fisher's more mechanical models of a free market. Judicial Officer Donald Campbell made just this point in his ruling on Henner's transactions, citing the case of Washington D.C. speculator Ralph W. Moore and the faked news release about U.S. Department of Agriculture edible oils purchases he had distributed in an effort to move lard futures prices. Moore's had been a crude effort, easy to debunk because the release did not have the usual U.S.D.A. letterhead. Campbell, however, used Moore's case to make the point that manipulation could involve acts other than a market corner—control of all or most of a commodity or the overall open position in a future—rather than to argue that Henner's moves to buy the board and then call out his limit up deal were fraudulent, as Moore's effort had been.[3] Fraud, after all, is rooted in dishonest information: the open outcry in the shell egg futures pit meant Henner had to say, in all honesty, that he really wanted a November future at 41.85 cents, whatever his motivation might have been. Whatever was going on in the shell egg futures pit was not the back and forth of Farmers Judson and Pratt or Steinbeck's used car lot owner and the farmer, or Moore's futures market version of the used car dealer who puts sawdust in an engine to hide the sound of worn, rattling parts. It was the sudden, inexplicable action of an individual, that only made sense to true believers in a market if seen as manipulation.

The reason for that conclusion is that faith in the kind of market that Walras and Fisher (and many others) proposed assumes there is nothing personal going on in a competitive market, as the economist Milton Friedman wrote a few years before David Henner called out his 41.85 cent bid. "There is no personal rivalry in the competitive market place. There is no personal higgling," he wrote, for in a free market, traders do not see themselves as personal rivals, even though they are all competitors, for "All take prices as given by the market."[4] Yet for John Hoekstra in the shell egg futures pit on June 25, 1968, things did feel personal. Hoekstra believed Henner had cut him off from filling three orders from a distant client.

In blackboard trading, brokers called out their bids and offers, which Mercantile Exchange employees posted on the separate bid and offer blackboards. They stuck a deal when they could match a bid to the lowest posted offer or an offer to the highest posted bid. On June 25, there had been no such match for forty minutes. Hoekstra's client orders were different; as "stop loss" orders they were not posted and only became buy orders after the prices hit a specified trigger. Hoekstra, then, was watching to see if the lowest offers on the board, one for 40.2 cents, one for 40.25 cents and one for 40.5 cents, found matching bids, at which point his client's first two stop loss orders became market orders to buy. After the first of the three 40.75 cent offers, he eyed the remaining two 40.75 cent posted offers, as well as a 41 cent offer and another for 41.3 cents as ways to complete his third client order. By buying the board, Henner cut him off. It was, perhaps, no wonder that he was a bit keyed up.[5]

Ill feeling brought another personal response: Henner simply gave Hoekstra three of his contracts: for Hoekstra's two 40.5 contracts, Henner handed over his 41 cent future and his 41.3 cent future, for the 40.65 cent contract, he handed over the 41.85 cent deal. If Henner had instead turned over three lower-priced contracts they would have allowed Hoekstra's clients to close out their shorts at lower prices, assuming Hoekstra used those futures to complete the stop-loss orders. At the close of trading that day, he had a choice of sticking his clients with a bigger loss than they had hoped or telling them he had missed a chance to fill their orders as directed.

The extremely personal gesture of giving away three contracts bothered Judicial Officer Donald Campbell, especially since Henner had turned over the limit-up contract. It was as if Henner posted a price without bothering to really complete a deal. As Hoekstra fumed, Mercantile Exchange executive vice president Kenneth B. McKay stepped up to tell Henner he was bothered, too, and would refer the matter to the exchange's board. McKay told Henner his dealings could look like a manipulation, but he himself was not sure. The exchange's board, however, ever mindful of the market's somewhat uncertain reputation, was. The board merely fined Henner for impairing the dignity of the market by giving away the contracts. As an afterthought, the board added "that he [Henner] spirited a market, jumping over prices ... which is also frowned upon, also considered bad practice." It did not sanction him for this, however.[6]

Henner explained his final, limit-up bid as what he felt he needed to secure the one last contract he wanted that day—though why he wanted nine contracts, rather than eight, he never clearly said. For Campbell, the point was that Henner's gift to Hoekstra showed that Henner really was not interested in buying that final future. Henner was trying to accomplish something else, and the timing, a bid right at the closing bell revealed his intention, Campbell argued. What Henner wanted, that is, was to set the closing price—and if King had not hit the bid, newspapers and price reporting agencies still would have reported the June 25 close as 41.85 cents. Campbell also felt it was particularly telling that Henner made no effort to replace any of three contracts he had given away that the next morning, June 26, when the price of the November future opened at 40.50, down 1.35 cents.

Doing a deal then would have been a less expensive way of staking out the same sixty-eight contract long position Henner said he had been so anxious to secure—so anxious that he had, he said, felt he needed to make that one last, limit up 41.85 cent bid to secure that last necessary future. With his 41.85 cent deal on June 25, Henner "would have us believe that he was so eager to have the ninth contract (which would raise his position to 68 contracts) that he bid 55 points higher than the highest price he had just paid (41.30) and 165 points higher than the lowest price he had just paid (40.20)," Campbell wrote. "If [Henner] was really so anxious to buy nine November shell egg futures on June 25, instead of eight, that he was willing to pay 41.85 to be sure of getting the ninth why did he not replace, at a lower price on June 26, the three contracts that he transferred to Mr. Hoekstra?" Campbell asked.[7]

Henner was not at the exchange that next day, but he could have telephoned an order in, Campbell noted. Henner was, however, back on

June 27, the day after, but all he did that day was to buy two November contracts at 40.45 cents and sold them two contracts at 40.40,—scalping, or making a quick deal for a quick profit. That left his position still at sixty five long futures, where it was after he gave the three contracts away. Yet he still did not move to replace the three contracts he had given to Hoekstra even though he could have done so for prices anywhere between 40.25 cents to 40.65 cents.[8]

Securing three replacement contracts at lower prices, however, would have undercut what Campbell argued was Henner's real intent: to send a price signal to speculators who were not able to watch the moment-by-moment dealing in the pit but who instead looked only at closing prices to get a sense of the market trend. By not replacing them, Campbell argued, Henner gave up the possibility of making an additional profit if the market touched the 50 cent price that Henner said he believed the November future would reach, whether he really thought and as in fact it never did.[9] The only reason that the transfer made sense, Campbell guessed, was to quiet Hoekstra's complaining and create some good will, though it is far from clear that giving away the highest price contracts would have done that. The personal touch, futures market-style, as it were.

The personal touch could also be a way of hiding intention—and to hide what you were doing had long been a feature of egg futures trading. The tight little circle of the egg futures brokers who knew each other so well (the kind of insiders who Mark Geiger argues are so often the actors who can disrupt financial markets pricing) had created a market that was, it seems, particularly easy to move, even though there were enough traders and enough action to look like a free and competitive market.[10] "I used to say three housewives could get together on the weekend and corner the egg market," Chicago Mercantile Exchange chairman Leo Melamed once joked.[11] Four years before Henner made his move, the 74 January 1964 frozen egg futures that broker Sidney Maduff and traders from The Siegel Company exchanged at a price of 30.25 cents a dozen were enough to move that contract to an artificial level.[12] Between November 10 and November 18, 1958 Berkshire Foods Inc. brokers Harold Fox and Earl Barnes orchestrated a squeeze involving themselves and several customers, with a long position that grew from 16 November futures to 424, forcing the price up by four cents a dozen as shorts tried to cover their positions.[13]

Traders can be inclined, as well, to the very human failing of hubris—especially those who, like Henner, made a bit of short term profit bucking market wisdom, as he had when he netted somewhere between $860 and $1,284 on his February trades—almost all of which he held for less than two weeks with a $7,000 margin payment making a profit of 12.3% to 18.3% on that speculation.[14]

Although the Department of Agriculture's April 11 *Poultry and Egg Situation* reported shipments of shell eggs were up by forty-five percent from the year before, that inventories of unsold fresh eggs were ninety percent higher and that the number of laying hens was still higher than 1967s usually large flock, Henner evidently took heart from the report's suggestion that egg prices might see substantial increases over 1967 levels from July on. Five days after the report's release, he staked out large, 28 contract long position. But the report, which typically qualified any forecast of prices, also warned that while a seventeen percent decline in the number of chicks hatched through the previous winter suggested there would be fewer hens laying eggs by next autumn, it said this was not certain because "the rate of culling may be tempered somewhat by a higher rate of forced molting," the still new technique that kept older hens laying more eggs over longer periods.[15]

Prices slid in the next few days after the release of the report, suggesting most traders looked at flock sizes and guessed that the U.S. Department of Agriculture's caution about culling and force-molting suggested that farmers might, taking to heart the department economists' forecasts of rising prices, might decide against taking hens out of production in the hopes that higher prices on a steady volume of shipments might make up for the losses they had suffered in 1967.[16] Henner's large long—his trades amounted to six percent of the April volume in the November future it would have accounted for nearly ten percent of all large speculators' long open position for all six egg futures (May, August, September, October November and December 1968) trading at the time. can came as other large players were covering their earlier longs.[17] Within days of this dramatic move by a closely-watched large player, shell egg futures began firming.

Confirmed in his view that he had read the April report correctly, when the next *Poultry and Situation* report, released June 12, again cautioned that while it expected supply to decline in the fall, the rate at which farmers culled older hens, or force-molted them and kept them laying "will have a strong bearing on flock size and egg production," he seems to have focused on the perhaps wishful thinking (which had characterized U.S.D.A. thinking on the outlook for a wide range of farm products) that "prices will likely average substantially above last fall's average of 30.1 cents a dozen." This was even more definitive than the "moderately to substantially" higher prices U.S.D.A. had floated as a possibility in the April report. Henner read this as confirming his bullish view—and acted.[18]

Still, while traders like to say, and maybe even think, that their bids and offers are based on reason and analysis—analysis that, because they are only human, is often informed more by hope than fact, as Henner's supposed analysis would have had to have been—it is not only impersonal acts that unfold in the trading pit, despite Friedman. The personal touch, moreover, is not only to be seen in traders' analyses: it could be about celebrating victory in the battle of buying and selling that the economist Herrell F. DeGraff had seen erupting even in supermarket aisles—and that perhaps Henner felt when palming off his contracts on Hoekstra.

The personal element in futures market gamesmanship, for instance, also emerged in a 1952, when it took a while for anyone else to see what was happening when Gilbert Miller, who ran the large egg wholesaler G.H. Miller Co, began buying December futures.[19] "The egg market has been a very erratic affair today and at this writing is showing pronounced strength," the December 17, 1952 Harris, Upham and Company *Closing Produce Letter* noted, as the December future's price rose to close at 39.77 cents on December 17 and rose again to close at 41.75 cents on the 18th. Despite selling that emerged after the early bump up in prices during the short open outcry session (after 9:45 a.m., buying and selling shifted to bids and offers posted on the egg pit blackboard), "At the decline, aggressive buying came in through a broker with merchandising connections who absorbed heavy offerings," the *Letter* noted. The next day, the firm's *Closing Produce Letter* reported that "The egg market has shown sustained strength all day, buying appearing to be a continuation of the same character as that which advanced prices so sharply yesterday." By the end of the day, Miller's group had bought an additional 142 contracts, at a cost of $71,000 in "margin" deposits. Then, Miller stepped up the pressure.[20]

On December 19, Miller called another broker—again, trying to mask his group's efforts to corner the market—ordering him to buy all the contracts he could, up with just five basis points below the day's limit: the 43.75 cent price that would have halted trading under the exchange's rules intended to prevent speculative runs. The market that day closed just above Miller's cap, ending at 43.72 cents a dozen: "The same group that is believed to have been putting the market higher the past few days are still buyers again today," Merrill Lynch's daily market letter noted that day, but it ruled out the idea of market manipulation for "A good deal of this buying is predicated on the fairly well substantiated rumor that the Mexican government is taking from 20,000 to 25,000 cases of storage eggs and it was also rumored that 5,000 cases would be shipped out of Chicago today or tomorrow on this order."

At this point, Miller's group held 216 contracts for December eggs—promises to buy eggs, including 46 at prices up to 38.70 cents a dozen, 65 at prices between 38.70 cents and 39.77 cents, 77 at prices between 39.77 cents and 41.75 cents and 28 at prices between 41.75 and 43.72. Other traders held 134 uncovered shorts, probably representing promises to sell at prices more than 41 cents, as those who had hit earlier bids at lower levels likely would have already covered their positions. Those with open positions were either hoping for a break in the market before trading stopped on the 23rd, so that they would have to pay less for a countervailing long contact, or, looking at the unusual position that January futures were trading for less than December deliveries, and that, as Harris Upham reported, there were reportedly some 64,016 cases (133 car-lots) of stored eggs on hand in Chicago. December 22 and 23 were frenzied. Traders closed out 150 of the Miller group's long contracts at prices mostly between 45.75 and 47.75. Nevertheless, at the final bell, there were still 66 that had not been settled. It was at this point that another quiet operation of the Miller group, the rounding up of actual car-lots—not as many as Harris Upham thought there were in total but, as it turned out 99% of those that were, a total of 79.[21]

Morris Weinger, a broker with Sol Weinger Company who had burned before by a squeeze Miller engineered on the December 1947 egg future, and whose testimony about the squeeze nailed down the federal court ruling that would for more than two decades define what manipulation of commodity trading entailed, was one of the traders who still had open short positions after the 23rd.[22] On December 30, with just one day left to act, and hoping that any ill feeling from his testimony about the earlier squeeze had faded, Weinger called Miller hoping for a way out. "Gil," he said, "you know I am short two cars of eggs and I understand you are the only one who has the eggs for delivery. I would like to purchase." Miller replied: "Are you in this deal? Gee, I'm sorry you happen to be in it."

He was not sorry enough, however, to give Weinger a way out of the short squeeze, however. Miller said he wanted a cent over the December

23 closing price, or 48.5 cents a dozen. Weinger protested: "Gil, how can you demand such a price?" to which Miller replied, "Those are my instructions. I have to get a cent over the option," although in fact he was the one who assembled his clients to create the corner.[23] Weinger unhappily bought the eggs, paying a bit more than $15,000. All in all, the manipulation netted Miller and his clients, including four Iowa egg shippers and two Texas poultry dealers, an aggregate profit from their futures dealings of about $162,000 on an outlay of no more than $108,000 in margins paid for futures contracts (portions of margins were rebated as closing prices exceeded the price paid for the contact). But as for the price?—"I said, '48 and a half cents for storage eggs?'" Weinger recalled, "I said, 'That is ridiculous.' He said, 'How much do you think these eggs are worth?' I said, 'They are worth about 35, 36 cents, at the most 38 cents.' But inasmuch as I did not want to default, I bought two cars of eggs, which I feel I overpaid at least 12 cents a dozen for delivery on the Exchange."[24]

Notes

1. Daniel Defoe, *The Life and Adventures of Robinson Crusoe*, Chapter XV, para 5.
2. John Steinbeck, *The Grapes of Wrath* (New York: Random House, 1939), 87–88. The "unpleasantness of haggling" was bad for business for "fair dealing brings them customers; whereas none will return to buy of him by whom he has been once imposed upon," Benjamin Franklin concluded when a friend told him that after "cheapening some trifles" higgling with a shopkeeper she told him "she actually lost by everything she sold." Benjamin Franklin, "Veritas lux clarior" Busy Body No.10, in *Memoirs of Benjamin Franklin. Written by Himself, and Continued by His Grandson and Others* (New York: Derby & Jackson, 1859 [1735?]), 493.
3. Moore had a long position of 1.8 million pounds of lard in the October 1947, November 1947, December 1947, January 1948 and March 1948 futures. He distributed a faked press release falsely suggesting that the U.S. Department of Agriculture was planning to buy millions of pounds of lard with some $147 million of an allocation to support the prices of edible oils and peanuts, leaving copies with a broker at a nationwide firm that published widely-followed market reports on commodities, as well as at the

National Press Club and in the mailboxes of reporters using the U.S. Department of Agriculture press room. The release, lacking the usual U.S.D.A. letterhead was easily shown to be a fake when the broker and reporters for the Associated Press and Chicago Journal of Commerce tried to verify it In re Ralph W. Moore, 9 Agriculture Decisions 1299, 1313, affirmed, 191 F.2d 775 (D.C. Circuit Court of Appeals,1949) cited In re Henner, 1234.

4. Milton Friedman, *Capitalism and Freedom* (Chicago: University of Chicago Press, 1962), 119.

5. In re Henner, 1160–1161. The offers on the board were for one contact at 40.2 cents, one at 40.25 cents, one at 40.50 cents, three at 40.75 cents, one at 41 cents and one at 41.3 cents.

6. In re Henner, 1162, 1255.

7. Ibid., 1187–1188.

8. Ibid., 1188.

9. The 41 cent, 41.3 cent and 41,85 cent futures represented a promise to buy 54,000 dozen eggs for a total of $22,347. If Henner had bought three contracts at the 40.4 cent price around which prices June 26and June 27 ranged, they would have represented a promise to buy those eggs for $21,816. If the November future had reached the low end of the range Henner forecast of 50 cents a dozen—it never did—he would have netted about $531 more by replacing the three higher price contracts. Giving the contracts away, meant missing out on a $5,184 profit if the November future hit 50 cents, though it saved him $1,500 in margin deposits.

10. Mark W. Geiger, *Floor Rules: Insider Culture in Financial Markets* (New Haven: Yale University Press, 2024); Floor Rules: The Unwritten Code of the Exchange Mark W. Geiger Paper presented at the Society for the Advancement of Socio-Economics Annual Conference, July, 2014.

11. David Greising and Laurie Morse, *Brokers, Bag Men and Moles: Fraud and Corruption in the Chicago Futures Markets* (New York: Wiley, 1991), 76.

12. In re Sidney Maduff et al., Commodity Exchange Authority Docket 125 (1965) Complaint, 2–3, https://www.cftc.gov/sites/default/files/idc/groups/public/@lrceacases/documents/ceacases/maduff-jan1965-453.pdf.

13. In re Berkshire Foods, Harold W. Fox, Earl E. Barnes, Commodity Exchange Authority Docket 91 (1959) Complaint and Notice of Hearing, 2–3, https://www.cftc.gov/sites/default/files/idc/groups/public/@lrceacases/documents/ceacases/berkshire-nov 1959-571.pdf.

14. Jean Cushen, "Financialization in the Workplace: Hegemonic Narratives, Performative Interventions and the Angry Knowledge Worker," *Accounting, Organizations and Society*, Vol. 38, No. 4 (May 2013), 314–331.

15. *Poultry and Egg Situation*, April 1968, 5.

16. Table 17 "Closing Prices on Principal Markets, by Future, Semi-monthly," *Commodity Futures Statistics* (July 1967–July 1968), 39.

17. Table 4 "Monthly Volume of Trading on Principal Markets, by Future," Ibid., 14; Table 21 "Long and Short Commitments of Reporting and Nonreporting traders in Principal Markets, semi-monthly," Ibid., 49.

18. *Poultry and Egg Situation*, June 1968, 5–6.

19. *Annual Report of the Administrator of the Commodity Exchange Authority for 1953*, 18. The egg futures of the 1940s and 1950s se were futures in "storage" eggs—fresh eggs that wholesalers had already purchased, coating the shells in vegetable and then holding them in refrigerated warehouses near the Mercantile Exchange. They could keep for months that way, and typically were processed further by "egg-breaking" or frozen egg firms for use in industrial food processes. The shell egg, or fresh egg, contract Henner traded were an innovation of the 1960s intended to revive a shrinking and somewhat notorious market by tying the futures to a more perishable item.

20. In re G.H. Miller,15 Agriculture Decisions 1015 (1956), 1028–1029.

21. Ibid., 1024–1025.

22. Weinger's testimony in the 1947 squeeze is cited in Brief of the Great Western Food Distributors Co in Petition for Review of Order of the Secretary of Agriculture. April 19 1952, 61, 90. https://www.google.com/books/edition/Great_Western_Food_Distributors_Inc_V_Br/nzAZpIymTRcC?hl=en&gbpv=1 and at In re Great Western Distributors, Inc., Nathaniel E. Hess, Charles

S. Borden Thomas F. Haynes, and Hartley L. Harris, Respondents (Commodity Exchange Authority Docket 48) Report of the Referee, 7, https://www.cftc.gov/sites/default/files/idc/groups/public/@lrceacases/documents/ceacases/great-aug1950-741.pdf.

In this case, the U.S. Court of Appeals for the Seventh Circuit established the rule that held any action that that produced an artificial price was necessarily intentional. Great Western Food Distributors v Brannon 201 F 2nd 476 (U.S. Court of Appeals, 7th Circuit, 1953) 484. here, the issue was Miller's purchases of a large long position, which grew from 42 to 292 December 1947 contracts while staking out a matching short position in the January 1948 contract, aiming to widen the spread between the two contracts. In addition to profits from unwinding the December long position at an artificially high price, Miller had secured January shorts at high prices that he expected to cover with less expensive long contracts after the December contract expired.

23. The Seventh U.S. Circuit Court of Appeals, citing its decision in the 1947 manipulation case in which Miller's action and Weinger's testimony had established the precedent of what manipulation entailed, and recalling Weinger's protest to Miller in the 1952 squeeze, wrote that "a long chain of circumstances ... definitely established" that Miller did "act with the intent" that its long futures and tight control of sales from its inventory of real eggs would cause an artificial price increase. G.H. Miller Co. v United States, 260 F.2d 286 (7th U.S. Circuit Court of Appeals, 1958), 290.

24. In re G.H. Miller, 1034.

References

Annual Report of the Administrator of the Commodity Exchange Authority for 1953

Brief of the Great Western Food Distributors Co in Petition for Review of Order of the Secretary of Agriculture. April 19, 1952

Commodity Futures Statistics (July 1967–July 1968)

Great Western Food Distributors v Brannon 201 F 2nd 476 (U.S. Court of Appeals, 7th Circuit, 1953)

In re Berkshire Foods, Harold W. Fox, Earl E. Barnes, Commodity Exchange Authority Docket 91 (1959)

In re Great Western Distributors, Inc., Nathaniel E. Hess, Charles S. Borden Thomas F. Haynes, and Hartley L. Harris, Respondents (Commodity Exchange Authority Docket 48)

In re David G Henner, 30 Agricultural Decisions 1151

In re G.H. Miller,15 Agriculture Decisions 1015

In re Sidney Maduff et al, Commodity Exchange Authority Docket 125 (1965)

G.H. Miller Co. v United States, 260 F.2d 286 (7th U.S. Circuit Court of Appeals, 1958)

Poultry and Egg Situation, April 1968, June 1968

Cushen, Jean: "Financialization in the workplace: Hegemonic narratives, performative interventions and the angry knowledge worker," *Accounting, Organizations and Society*, Vol. 38, No. 4 (May 2013), 314–331

Friedman, *Capitalism and Freedom* (Chicago: University of Chicago Press, 1962)

Geiger, Mark: *Floor Rules: Insider Culture in Financial Markets* (New Haven: Yale University Press, 2024)

Greising, David and Laurie Morse: *Brokers, Bag Men and Moles: Fraud and Corruption in the Chicago Futures Markets* (New York: Wiley, 1991)

CHAPTER 6

The Intent of One, the Intentions of Two

Abstract A trader's intent was the central question about an artificial price. It was particularly important for regulators in the egg futures case, because a few years earlier, they had failed to convince a court that they had found a manipulation of the cotton market by the Volkart Brothers firm and a squeeze that generated an artificially high price. In the egg futures case, regulators aimed to rebut this, essentially by showing when and how Henner acted, and when and why he did not, was evidence of intent and therefore evidence of a manipulation to create an artificial price. Demonstrating intent would be the critical stumbling block in proving manipulation in derivatives trading; the complications of these markets and their apparent similarity to the theoretical ideal of free competitive market would also continue to frustrate efforts to define manipulation in statute.

Keywords Futures market · Intention · Artificial price · Market manipulation

In law, as in life, not every act is intentional. What, then, was David Henner's intention when he called out his 41.85 cent big for a single November egg future? What did any broker or trader intend when agreeing to a price that was out of line with the prevailing pattern in a market or with prices in a related market? When, then, was such a price an artificial one? A mistake? In an open outcry market like the shell egg futures trading pit, is the mere act of bidding—even bidding far more than anyone had been offering to sell, that 41.85 cents—in and of itself intent? Could it be simply reflex, an instantaneously, unconsidered and possibly unintentional reaction to … well, what? The reaction of others to Henner's buying the board? Awareness that the bell to close the session was about to sound?

For Judicial Officer Campbell, David Henner's artificial price with an intention to manipulate the November egg future was demonstrated when that out-of-line 41.85 cent bid followed so closely his move to buy the board at much lower prices, especially since Henner rarely bid for contracts but usually simply hit other traders' offers.[1] The question had become urgent by 1970, when Henner's case came before Campbell, because a legal standard established more than two decades earlier had recently been overturned by a federal appeals court ruling on an alleged manipulation in cotton futures. At the same time, the U.S. Department of Agriculture was again trying to move legislation through Congress that would more clearly define manipulation—which had never been formally defined in statute, and which so far still has not been—without quite being candid enough to admit that its aim was to overturn the cotton futures decision. In addition, and also at the same time, regulators wanted to fend off a court challenge to a much larger manipulation case, involving trading in a futures market with a much more direct impact on farm and consumer prices than either shell eggs or cotton—wheat—and involving a player with enormous power to dictate cash market prices for wheat and wholesale prices to millers. This case was pending in a different appeals court that the one that ruled on the cotton futures matter, and a conflicting decision here could keep the older legal standard for manipulation alive, or so Campbell and his colleagues hoped.

Before the cotton futures case, the legal standard for judging traders' intentions when agreeing on out-of-line futures price was to consider what the traders had done before striking a deal. This standard was set in the appeals court decision upholding the Commodity Exchange Authority's ruling that Great Western Food Distribution had manipulated the December 1947 egg future. In this case, the court found Great Western's intention was demonstrated by its accumulation of a large open position in the future just before the contracts' expiry while at the same time selling real eggs to out of town buyers so they were unavailable for shorts seeking to cover their positions.[2] In the case of the Swiss cotton merchant Volkart Brothers' dealings in October 1957 cotton futures on the New York and New Orleans Cotton Exchanges, it was the firm's large long position and the timing and pricing of its offers to liquidate that position that looked like manipulation to U.S. Department of Agriculture Judicial Officer Thomas Flavin, one of Campbell's colleagues.

Cotton futures trading was a bigger dollar value business than shell egg trading in 1968, but the number of contracts traded was significantly less: a grand total of 197 contracts traded in October 1957, the month in which the Commodity Exchange Authority alleged Volkart had manipulated the market, while only 1,062 traded over the life of the contract compared to the 733 November 1968 egg futures contracts traded just in June 1968. Over the life of a contract in some 54,116 contracts traded.[3] Cotton futures traders were apparently more expert, and certainly more closely connected to the market for actual bales of cotton, since hedgers—basically brokers with cotton to sell—accounted for 22.6% of trading in long contracts, while hedgers looking to offset the risk of rising cash prices accounted for 32.2%; in the shell egg market, hedgers accounted for 0.4% of the longs and 4.7% of short contract trades.[4] Still, the direct connection to transactions in eggs or cotton was about the same, with 0.5% of cotton futures clear with the delivery of real bales versus 0.3% of shell egg futures.[5] With more trades and probably many more traders—the lower cost of egg futures attracting the small speculators who accounted for more than 72% of long shell egg futures trades in 1968 and more than 77% of shorts in 1968, compared to 58% and 55% for cotton in 1957—the relatively more active egg futures market was closer to the markets of Friedman's or von Mises' or Walras' or Fisher's models than was the cotton futures market.

By early autumn in 1957, the Swiss cotton merchant Volkart Brothers held by far the largest open position on the New York Cotton Exchange, with 197 long October futures, representing 19,700 bales or 9.85 million pounds of notional cotton. On September 24, the first day that shorts could give notice that they intended to deliver real bales of cotton to close their open positions, Volkart began liquidating its longs, reducing its position to 12,700 bales by October 1, at which point Volkart's New York trader then posted an offer to sell 10 contracts at 34.97 cents a pound—1.87 cents above the spot price, at which bales of real cotton were actually trading—and waited.[6]

Nobody hit this offer; it was too high a price. But on October 10, Volkart directed its New York broker to post offers to sell another 40 contracts at prices stepping up from 35.02 cents to 35.15; these, too, were ignored. On Monday, October 14, the day before the October future expired, Volkart's broker at the company's direction posted another offer to sell 10 contracts at 35.22 cents as well as an offer to sell 64 contracts at 35.27 cents. The market's shorts began to get the message: the largest long in the market was not going to let them cover their positions for less than the 34.20 to 34.50 cents a pound they had expected to pay, based on the usual relation difference between cash price and prices for a future nearing expiry. Volkart sold 20 contracts, 2,000 bales, at 34.97 and 35.02 that day.[7] By October 14, meanwhile, Volkart's agent on the smaller New Orleans Cotton Exchange covered a short position of 16 October futures then then established an open long position of 17 October futures, in effect increasing the cotton or cotton futures shorts would have to deliver by 3,300 bales.[8]

All in all, on the morning of Tuesday, October 15, the day that both the New York and New Orleans October futures expired and therefore the day that all the traders would have to close open position with offsetting futures or notices they would deliver real bales of cotton, Volkart's 104 October long futures in New York accounted for 89% of that exchanges total open position; its 17 New Orleans longs for 97% of that market's total open position. On that date where were only 4,963 bales of cotton certified as satisfying the quality and delivery standards of the Cotton Exchanges' contracts: 500 pounds of "middling one-inch" cotton, with staple lengths between 29/32nds of an inch to 1-1/6 inch, in warehouses at New York, New Orleans, Mobile, Alabama, Houston or Galveston, Texas.[9] Over the same two weeks in October that Volkart was liquidating some of its longs, other traders sold another 170 contracts, promising to deliver 17,000 bales or buy 170 long October contracts by October 15—and the only place they could find anything close to that number of October futures for sale was Volkart.[10] Everyone in the business, meanwhile, was aware of the size of Volkart's positions.[11]

Early on the morning of October 15, Volkart ordered its broker on the New York Cotton Exchange to sell 20 October futures at 35.17 cents a pound, and then to close the rest of its long position by offering 84 short contracts at 35.27 cents a pound. As shorts scrambled to cover positions, the broker did manage to sell the 20 contracts at 35.17 cents along with 34 more at the 35.27 cents, and by the end of the day, Volkart received notices that the buyers would deliver approximately 5,000 bales to clear the rest of its long position.[12] Later that morning, before the start of trading on the New Orleans Cotton Exchange, Volkart directed its broker there to liquidate its 17 long October futures at not less than 35.38 cents per pound, and to take delivery of any part of the said position which could not be sold at this price or better. The firm's New Orleans broker sold 16 futures at prices ranging from 35.40 to 35.48 cents per pound and later than day, Volkart received notices of delivery of approximately 100 bales.[13] In the end, Volkart received 5,100 bales on October 22. Two months later, on December 19, it redelivered 3,707 of these bales to clear its short position in the December 1957 future on the New Orleans exchange.[14]

Just as Judicial Officer Donald Campbell would note nine years later looking at David Henner's egg futures trading and how the November future close on June 25 compared with the October and December futures, Thomas J. Flavin, the Judicial Officer hearing the Volkart case, was struck by the unusually wide price spread between the October 1957 and December 1957 cotton future. On October 11, the Friday before Volkart's push to liquidate its longs, the New York October future traded above the December contract by 0.56 cents a pound, while the New Orleans October over December spread was 0.39 cents. As shorts hit Volkart's 35-plus cent offers on October 14 and in the bulk of the deals on October 15, the October over December spread widened to 0.92 cents in New York and 1.12 cents in New Orleans, Flavin reported. These were larger than any October to December spread at expiry seen in the previous ten years or in the year after, he added.[15]

Unlike Campbell, Flavin also looked at the price of the actual commodity the contracts proposed to exchange. This was necessary because, unlike Henner in the egg futures pit, where he was simply a speculator who dealt only in futures and was uninvolved with the commerce in real eggs, Volkart actually bought and sold bales of cotton and from time to time would use long futures to acquire real bales or deliver real bales from its inventory to close a short position. As of October 11, Volkart had 33,291 bales of cotton in its inventory and earmarked for sale in the United States; it had sales commitments in hand for 30,900 bales. On Monday, October 14, it bid 33.31 cents a pound for 740 bales of cotton offered for sale by the Commodity Credit Corporation, a federal price stabilization agency, with other purchases, by the end of that day it had 41,000 bales of cotton in hand or on its way to a warehouse, and sales commitments for 39,900.[16] It boosted this with additional cash purchases on October 15, the same day it was selling the bulk of its long futures, to 44,269 bales. The unusually wide spread between different futures, whether the November to October and November to December shell egg future or the October to December cotton future was one sign of an artificial price to Judicial Officers Campbell and Flavin. The spread between futures and cash price in the case of Volkart's cotton trading signaled something additional, on top of a false price, to Flavin: intent.

The reason for this is what Volkart executives said they were doing. Alfred Boedtker, the company's New York-based president, told a Commodity Exchange Authority hearing that the company had no intention of moving prices of the future but was simply trying to hedge against its cash market sales. Karl Muller, Volkart's New Orleans-based vice president, testified that Volkart had built its large long position as part of a routine hedging operation against sales commitments of spot cotton. He said he based the selling price offers on what Volkart was paying to buy real bales at inland points, although the Commodity Exchange Authority investigators found the spot price of actual cotton sales at Memphis, Tennessee ranged between 32.80 and 33.20 through the second half of September and the whole of October.[17] But the more than 35-cent sales price Volkart quoted and that shorts eventually had to take, was well above the normal one cent a pound premium over cash prices where cotton futures usually traded in the final month before expiry, Flavin said. On the Friday before Volkart's big sales moves, at those 35-plus cent a pound prices, the New York future traded at 1.39 cents and the New Orleans future at 1.2 cents above the average cash price at New Orleans, Houston and Galveston, Texas, the three primary delivery points. As Volkart completed its deals on October 15, the future's expiry, when the need to cover positions was most urgent, this spread widened to 1.92 cents for the New York future and 2.13 cents in New Orleans. These were far larger premiums for the future than Flavin could track at any point for the ten previous years or for the year after. They were, in fact, twice the size of most other year's spreads, he noted.[18]

The price was also well above what Volkart was paying to buy real cotton. Between October 15 and October 22, when the firm took delivery of the 5,100 bales that shorts in New York and New Orleans delivered to close their positions, Volkart bought an additional 17,635 bales on the cash market, where prices ranged from 33.2 to 33.5 cents

a pound. Even with the additional sales of its stockpiled cotton it nego-
tiated during that week, all for delivery over the following six months,
Volkart still held an inventory of nearly 6,600 bales of cotton available
for domestic sale—factoring in its worldwide inventory and worldwide
sales commitments and that balance was nearly 59,000 bales. It had no
need for long futures as hedge against the risk it might have to buy real
cotton at high prices in the future. Volkart's "trading in cotton futures
during October 1957 did not constitute hedging," Flavin said. "At all
times between September 23 and October 8, 1957, it had a long fixed
price position and also a long futures position. Such positions constituted
speculation in spot cotton and futures."[19]

Generally speaking, market regulators were less concerned when individuals and firms actively trading an actual commodity acquired large
open positions as a hedge than when speculators did. Volkart's futures
position and stockpiled bales of cotton showed it could have easily cleared
its open futures or sold some of its inventory that had not already been
committed to shorts, who would then in effect redeliver it to Volkart. On
the other hand, even a firm actively trading the actual commodity can be
acting in the role of speculator when its futures position is not effective
insurance against the risk of an adverse price more, as U.S. Department of
Agriculture analysts demonstrated three decades before Volkart's trading
with their analysis of two large grain buyers' overwhelming large short
position in the December 1926 wheat future. That speculation drove
down the cash price at harvest time; covering the costs sent the price
of the future soaring, yielding both a nice profit to the two firms and
a higher cash price as they started selling their inventory of wheat to
millers.[20]

The 35.17 cents and 35.27 cents per pound Volkart secured for its
New York futures and the 35.38 cents or better it received for its New
Orleans contracts pushed the price of the New York October future up
from its Monday October 14 close to 34.91 cents a pound bid and 35.03
cents asked (suggesting that a deal could have been made, though it was
not, at the 34.97 cents midpoint) to the Tuesday cost at 35.27 cents, the
price Volkart was insisting upon. The New Orleans future moved even
more, from 34.60 cents bid to close that final trading day at 35.48 cents;
Volkart's directive to sell its New Orleans future at 35.38 or better netted
it that better price.[21] "Why did this happen? The answer is inescapable,"
Flavin wrote: Volkart's long position was more than twice the size of
the supply of actual cotton certified as meeting the contract's quality and

delivery specifications. At the start of the day on Tuesday, October 15, the last day anyone could buy or sell futures and the deadline by which they had to clear their positions, the open positions on both exchanges totaled 134 contracts for 13,400 bales of cotton, including Volkart's combined New York and New Orleans long position of some 12,100 bales. Traders needing to close their positions had few options other than to deal with Volkart: there were just 4,963 bales of real cotton certified as meeting the future's strict quality and warehouse specifications, and only 13 contracts that other longs had available for sale. They would not get much of a break there: On the New York exchange, E.F. Hutton & Company told its trader to offer its four long futures, for just 400 bales, a one- or two- one hundredths of a cent below Volkart's offer that day. "Professional traders recognized the obvious fact that a concentrated long would make or determine market prices for cotton futures on that day," Flavin wrote.[22]

In the week after the October future expired, traders with short positions had had to buy long futures to offset some 70 short futures, for some 7,000 bales. There was no place else to go except for Volkart. "The futures prices were therefore artificial as brought about by technical factors within the futures market itself and not by any supply or demand factors for cotton generally or by free trading opinion as to such factors," Flavin concluded, adding: "This is true regardless of what spot cotton prices were." Meanwhile, Volkart's purchases of cotton on the cash market would be in his view critical evidence of intention to manipulate the futures market. What happened on the New York and New Orleans exchanges on October 15, 1957 was a squeeze, pure and simple, Flavin ruled. The New York Cotton Exchange's argument, in defense of Volkart, that the jump in the October future that day simply reflected demand and supply of futures contracts—not cotton—was "patently lacking in merit" since accepting that view "would justify as valid corners, 'squeezes' and all kinds of manipulation both up and down," Flavin wrote—just as Campbell dismissed the notion that just because David Henner and Marlowe King struck a deal at 41.85 cents a dozen for the November shell egg future, they had somehow found a real, rather than an artificial, price.[23]

But striking a deal at an unreal price, on its own, is not manipulation. It can be, as Dee Belveal testified in support of Henner, simply bad judgement or a mistake: a glitch that a free market can correct, as Belveal noted the egg futures market did the day after Henner's 41.85

cent deal. To make his case that Henner manipulated the market, Campbell looked at the pattern of his trading, as well as the same futures market price patterns that Flavin did: in Henner's case, the November egg future's price movements over the previous days and the spread between November and October and December futures, while Flavin looked at the October cotton futures price trend and at the spread between October and December futures. Wide spreads between futures were particularly telling in both judicial officers' view.

To show intent, Campbell detailed Henner's timing; Flavin at whether Volkart's trading could have in any way hedged any risk it faced in its business of dealing in real cotton. He noted that, through October, Volkart was buying cotton on the cash market—cotton to delivered on the spot or within a few days—at prices roughly six percent below where it was pricing its futures and in amounts far larger than its open position in futures. With that much low-priced cotton in its inventory, the risk Volkart needed to insure itself against was the risk that prices would fall when it needed to sell that cotton; if cash prices fell and the futures followed, Volkart's futures market position would have lost money, not served to offset losses in the cash market. Moreover, Flavin wrote, almost all of Volkart's cash purchases of cotton from mid-September through October was for cotton with a staple length longer than one inch—longer than the cotton specified in the futures contract—and that much of what it bought was of a higher grade than the middling cotton of the futures contracts. The "explanation that Volkart held its October long contracts into October 15 for delivery of cotton because it was experiencing difficulty in getting the higher quality spot cotton it wanted and sought to get it through deliveries on its futures contracts is simply not credible," Flavin wrote.[24]

Flavin brushed off another argument from the New York Cotton Exchange that because the price increases in the October future were not very large, the price had not been manipulated. The exchange argued that if a trader or firm with a controlling long position holds out for too high a price, even if certificated stocks of cotton were not large enough to satisfy those long contracts, cotton merchants would see a chance to profit by entering the market as shorts and then delivering cotton at a profit. Until prices reach the trigger (the "bother" price) for this move, the exchange said longs should be able to profit at the expense of shorts already in the market who had (in the exchange's view) "overstayed" by not previously clearing their position. To this, Flavin replied that "It seems elementary and beyond controversy that the deliberate pressuring of futures prices upward by a 'squeeze' technique resulting in artificial or fictitious prices intentionally brought about constitutes manipulation of price." He added that "It is no answer to say that prices were not substantially, unreasonably or excessively raised." The issue was not whether October cotton futures prices were too high or unreasonable, but simply whether they had been manipulated. "Small manipulations as well as large manipulations are prohibited by the [Commodity Exchange] Act," he wrote.[25] For Flavin, the only explanation for Volkart's directives to its brokers on the New York and New Orleans exchanges was that it "sought to raise October future prices on such exchanges."[26] He suspended Volkart and its executives from trading for fifteen days.[27]

Volkart appealed, though this penalty was even less than the 30 days suspension that Henner, nine years later, decided that it was not worth worrying about. Yet while the Commodity Exchange Authority had long felt that federal appeals court decisions in cases challenging earlier decisions finding squeezes like Volkart's were manipulations, the agency was to receive a shock in this case—one which Campbell tried to address with his ruling on Henner's egg futures deals. For, after reciting, word for word, several hundred word of a primer on futures markets submitted by the New York Cotton Exchange in its amicus curiae brief supporting Volkart (filling two two-column pages of the published opinion),[28] Fifth Circuit Court of Appeals Judge Richard Rives accepted the central argument the Exchange made to Flavin: that is was perfectly legitimate for a long to push prices higher if shorts had not acted in time to clear their positions.

For the Exchange, and Judge Rives, it was simply the workings of the free market, the resolution of demand and supply for futures contracts. The fact that cotton merchant members of the Exchange—firms that held stockpiles of cotton (as, indeed Volkart did)—did not come into the market in response to Volkart's offering prices, the free market response to an artificially high price, proved that those prices were not unreal, the Exchange argued and Rives accepted. The $1,833,040 of New York futures sales Volkart completed on October 15 were only $21,230 more than it would have received if it had completed those sales the day before, Rives noted.[29] (Volkart's New Orleans sales would have yielded at least another $300,730. Altogether this sum was some $64,670 more than the normal one cent spread over the spot price would have yielded; if the firm were hedging its inland cotton purchases, which Muller said he was basing his offer prices on, this was $149,370 over the late-September Memphis price, or a 7.5% premium.)[30] Flavin had argued that to assume the theoretical free market response that merchants would step in if they say the price was out of line with demand and supply was to simply say it was not possible to create an artificial price., squeezes and corners and other manipulations were perfectly legitimate. Here, Flavin prefigured Campbell's analysis of Henner's transactions.

It was not only the small (if understated) gap between October 14 and October 15 prices that mattered, Rives continued. Volkart and the New York Cotton Exchange, Rives wrote, "emphasize the fact that there were millions of bales of cotton available in the Country," including 1.25 million bales in port warehouses designed as delivery points under the Exchange's contract specifications. While these bales were not certificated—officially verified as meeting the contracts' quality and weight standards—Volkart and the Exchange "insist that the shorts, through their brokers, could have obtained cotton at the ports and placed it in process of certification on October 13 or 14th," the judge wrote.[31] He cited no other evidence for this. In fact between October 15 and October 22, shorts were able to buy and certify very few bales; a total of just 137, based on the delivery data that Flavin tracked.[32] Flavin ruled that the uncertificated cotton was not readily available (as well as that the cotton Volkart was actively buying on the cash market at the time was of a significantly different standard than the futures contract specified).

Rives disagreed. Though he noted that nearly a quarter of the 5,100 bales Volkart received came from shorts' existing inventories "it is nonetheless true that all of the shorts had the same opportunity."[33] Shorts, that is, not only had enough time to acquire bales and obtain necessary certifications but for many, doing so meant getting started well before October 15; the one point seems to almost contradict the other, as well as Rives' stern conclusion that "Unless the shorts are to be excused from the performance of their contracts and from the exercise of due diligence to that end, the ample supply of uncertificated cotton must be considered as available to them."[34] The only path to conclude Volkart had intentionally manipulated the market was "upon the assumption that the shorts should not be held to their contract obligation to deliver the cotton," Rives wrote.[35] Here, he insisted on the connection of futures with real cotton, even if of potentially different cotton than the contract specified, and the Exchange's argument that it was the supply and demand of futures contracts, not cotton, that justified the October

15 price rise.[36] Rives concluded that to say that shorts should not be required to deliver cotton with the expiry of the future—which Flavin had not said—would be to put the Commodity Exchange Authority "in the position of regulating a gambling institution rather than a legitimate futures exchange."[37]

This ruling was what Judicial Officer Campbell wanted to challenge. Henner had raised the Volkart decision as a defense against the Authority's manipulation charge, prompting Cambell to attach a 27-page appendix to his unusually lengthy, 113-page opinion in the case.[38] There was, in addition, a much bigger case the background at the time: a pending challenge by Cargill Inc., to another Commodity Exchange Authority manipulation ruling, that the Authority worried would end up confirming Volkart. In this case, Judicial Officer Thomas Flavin (the same Judicial Officer who decided the Volkart case) noted that Cargill argued "the ruling in Volkart is to the effect that intentional squeezes are not manipulation in violation of the act," but that "we, of course, do not agree."[39] As Campbell outlined, at length, his own analysis of the Commodity Exchange Authority's view of the Volkart decision, one of the biggest and most politically influential grain traders of all had gone to court to argue that the Volkart decision gave it cover for its market moves.

The Cargill case involved wheat futures. With the spring 1963 harvest of soft red winter wheat, the variety used for cookie and cake flour, looked to be more than enough to meet millers' demand, Cargill decided to hedge the large inventory it already had in hand. It did so in the classic way, by selling May futures on the Chicago Board of Trade, taking out a short open position of 8 million bushels. If cash wheat prices fell, Cargill would offset any losses when selling stockpiled grain by gains from unwinding its shorts. But in February and March, Cargill sold substantial quantities of soft red winter wheat to mills in the Southwestern part of the United States, which was not a normal market for it because rail freight rates normally meant this was no an economic option: soft red winter wheat was grown mainly in southern Illinois, western Kentucky, Wisconsin, western Ohio and tidewater Maryland and Virginia. A temporary, low-cost rail connection briefly opened this market, and at the same time the Spanish government indicated it was in the market for a large amount of soft red winter wheat: soft red wheat prices were unusually high.[40]

Rather than a large harvest looking to depress prices, Cargill executives now believed supply would be tight and that prices would rise by the time all the crop was in, that May. Cargill's traders began gradually liquidating their short positions, completing this on April 15, at which point they also staked out a 250,000-bushel long position. By May 15, they had increased Cargill's long position to 1,930,000 bushels, just short of the maximum speculative position Board of Trade rules allowed (a hedge was not subject to this limit).[41] Everyone else around the wheat pit, meanwhile, was reassured by an April 12 U.S. Department of Agriculture report that there were 2,804,000 bushels of deliverable soft red winter wheat in Chicago warehouses—what they apparently did not know was that Cargill owned 2,471,000 bushels of that supply. When Spain announced it would buy soft red winter wheat, Cargill on May 14 struck deals for 500,000 bushels at $2.13-1/2, which was 10-1/2 cents above the May future (which at this point was converging on cash price). On May 15, it sold another 600,000 bushels at $2.09, or 5-1/2 cents above the future that day. It loaded 770,000 bushels from its Chicago warehouses, supplying the rest from facilities in Spain. With existing commitments for 1,651,000 bushels at that point, it had as of May 15, just 50,000 bushels on hand—it would arrange the sale of these on May 16. The squeeze was on.[42]

Other traders began sensing that the market was tightening. On Friday, May 17, the May future closed higher at $2.09-3/8 a bushel. Under the Board of Trade's rules, the maximum the future could rise on Monday was $2.19-3/8 and Cargill ordered its broker to sell 100,000 bushels at $2.19, but the broker could not complete the deal. The May future closed that day at $2.18-5/8. On May 21, the last day the May future could be traded, it opened at $2.22 but gradually declined to a low $2.15-1/4 by around 11 a.m. With an hour to go before trading ended, the price bounced back to $2.20, at which point Cargill directed its broker to close out its open position, with six orders: one to sell 200,000 bushels at $2.27, then 200,000 bushels at $2.27-1/4; 300,000 bushels at $2.27-1/2; 400,000 bushels at $2.27-3/4; 500,000 bushels at $2.28 and 390,000 bushels at $2.28-1/4. This approach of making several sales orders at stepped up prices, called scale-pricing or step-up orders, can be a way to tap a rising trend in price—or to create one. By 11:53 am, a tick up in the wheat future price began triggering these sell orders, and Cargill's broker liquidated 1,625,000 bushels of the company's open long position. In the confused and frenzied trading in those final minutes, contracts for some 420,000 bushels remained open.[43]

After a visit from the acting chairman of the Board of Trade's business conduct committee, Cargill said it would agree to settle traders' open short position by selling them warehouse receipts at $2.28-1/4 a bushel. This cleared 370,000 bushels of the short open interest; other longs sold receipts to settle the rest; shorts then redelivered these receipts to Cargill, which allowed it to clear most of its own open long position of 365,000 bushels. In all these paper exchanges, a grand total of 50,000 bushels of real wheat ended up changing hands.[44] "At 11:45, the time when Cargill placed its sale order, [the May wheat future] was trading at $2.20, which was about 1-1/2 cents over the previous day's close," wrote Judge John Gibson of the U.S. Circuit Court of Appeals for the Eight Circuit. "In other words, throughout the day prior to Cargill's last-minute sale the market was resistant to any further increase in the price of the future. Cargill's sell order was at prices 7 and 8 cents over what the future was then selling for," Judge Gibson continued. "It seems clear that the only reason the price advanced so rapidly during the last few minutes of trading was because of Cargill's dominance of the long interest and the high prices it set for liquidation."[45]

That circumstantial evidence, in the absence of any admission from Cargill, was enough to prove manipulation. Nevertheless, "Aside from the obvious inferences to be drawn from the objective facts in this case," Judge Gibson noted, "there is other evidence in the record which shows that Cargill knew exactly what was going on." That included a May 6, 1963, inter-office telegram reading: "Excellent wheat summary. Question is how much wheat going to be available June 15 so we can figure old crop needs and what it going to cost our pals."[46] Cargill's main argument, that the shorts had a responsibility to deliver wheat or buy futures—the New York Cotton Exchange argument that swayed Judge Rives in the Volkart case—did not convince Judge Gibson. He rejected Cargill's argument that it had not in effect cornered the soft red winter wheat supply with its combination of stockpiled wheat and open position in the long future because that traders with short positions had another option than to deal with Cargill, the argument that in the Volkart decision led Judge Rives in the 5th Circuit to hold that Volkart Brothers had not manipulated cotton prices. In the Cargill case, that option was supposedly to buy and deliver hard red winter wheat, which "is of a higher quality and price than soft red winter wheat, is rarely delivered on the contract, and no premium is allowed if it is," Judge Gibson said.[47] Although commodity exchanges' rules allowing delivery of a similar physical commodity that does not match the specifications of quality or delivery points of a futures contract are intended as a way to prevent market corners, Gibson's view was that high-protein, high gluten hard winter wheat, used for bread and pasta, was not really a substitute for low-protein, low-gluten soft wheat, used for cakes and confectionaries, and in any event that Cargill was not entitled to claim a premium.

The apparent conflict over the two Circuit Appeals Courts' differing views what the responsibility of shorts in a futures market entailed, and therefore whether a firm with a large long position had manipulated a market or simply marked up its sales offer to an appropriate free market level would not be resolved. In one sense, it came down to whether uncertificated cotton could be acquired and certified within the time frame allowed by commodity exchanges' rules versus whether hard red winter wheat could be delivered to clear a soft red winter wheat contract. The conflict between the two appeals court interpretations of similar situations was also hard to resolve because in addition to the circumstantial evidence Judge Gibson relied on to show Cargill intended to move the wheat future price by manipulating the market, he cited a Cargill that set down that intent in an executive's own words.

The Supreme Court was not interested in the issue. What manipulation was and when it could be shown, remained unclear for decades to come.[48] The issue, a later Commodity Futures Trading Commission chairman, Philip McBride Johnson, would note, was whether traders with a long position not intentionally created to create a squeeze can lawfully exact as high a price as possible, when traders trying to cover shorts find it is difficult or impossible to deliver the commodity in question. "Natural market congestion can occur without any effort on the part of the longs to create the shortage of cash supplies. For example, the court in Cargill noted that a scarcity might be occasioned by low crop production or the inadvertent destruction of existing supplies," Johnson noted, in a 1982 opinion. "Some commentators have read Volkart as saying that longs are free to demand the highest possible prices from shorts under these circumstances, whereas the Cargill decision assailed such conduct."[49]

Congress, too, balked at tackling the question of defining manipulation. Two years before Henner's egg market dealing, and in the aftermath of Anthony DiAngelis's attempt to corner the soybean oil futures market with the help of fraudulent storage tank receipts and more than $100 million of bad loans,[50] the Department of Agriculture asked Congress to define manipulation "to mean the exacting, causing or maintaining of an abnormal or artificial price by any action or course of action which raises, depresses, fixes, pegs, or stabilizes the price at or to a level different than that which would otherwise prevail."[51] This definition would have made moot the Volkart decision holding that cotton market shorts could have found cotton to cover their positions was to blame for leaving such a large short uncovered for so long, for it added that creating an artificial price was manipulation "irrespective of any acts or omissions by the holders of futures contracts adversely affected thereby." If it had been enacted, this definition also would have made irrelevant the argument that since that Marlowe King was the willing buyer of David Henner's offer to sell a contract to buy November eggs at 41.85 cents a dozen, 41.85 cents was the real price of a November future contract at that instant.

"Is the purpose of this proposal to overrule the so-called Volkart decision?" Rep. Robert Dole, Republican of Kansas, asked during the House of Representatives subcommittee's hearings on the bill, brushing off the assertions of senior Department of Agriculture officials that this was not the aim. "[T]here must be an intent to influence price ... that factor is not included in your definition of 'manipulation'," Dole continued. "I think that you infer 'intent' very frequently from the action of the man as he knowingly does something, and if it has that result, why, 'intent' is inherent when you connect it to his action." The problem, University of Illinois economist Thomas A. Hieronymus testified, was that "Everyone who makes a trade, even the smallest job lot trader, has an effect on price and causes it to be something different than otherwise would have prevailed. Thus every trader would be guilty," he said.[52]

What about potatoes? asked Harry Graham, of the National Grange, the next witness before the subcommittee. Potato futures on the New York Mercantile Exchange had already been the subject of two major price manipulation cases in the eight years since the Commodity Exchange Authority began regulating the market, he said, and "The history of that market is that over a period of several years, the shorts controlled the market," Graham said.[53] The future was based on Irish, or white potatoes from Aroostook County, Maine, and by selling futures for far more potatoes than could be delivered to limited number of delivery points in that isolated stretch of northern Maine, speculators could push prices so low that they could easily close positions at a profit with low-priced longs. Those low prices were where buyers pegged cash prices to farmers across the nation, including states that produced more potatoes than Maine. Tightening the Commodity Exchange Act, Graham argued, would help markets find a real price: first, by, codifying a definition of price manipulation that did not require, as a recent court case had, direct rather than the circumstantial evidence of intent that, for instance, was how Judicial Officer Campbell would determine that Henner had manipulated the shell egg market. Amending the Act could also allow the Authority to bar futures trading in commodities where it was relatively easy to manipulate prices, he said. "I am convinced that a great deal of the high pricing of bacon at the present time is a result of speculation in pork bellies," Graham said. "There are not enough of pork bellies being traded to have established a market at the level they now have."[54]

Nor would there be, when Henner turned his attention to that market.

NOTES

1. In re Henner, 1187.
2. Great Western Foods v Brannon 201 F2d 476, 484 (U.S. Court of Appeals, 7th Circuit, 1953).
3. Calculated from Table 4 "Monthly Volume of Trading in Principal Markets, by Future" *Commodity Futures Statistics* (July 1956–July 1957), 17; *Commodity Futures Statistics* (July 1957–July 1958), 17; *Commodity Futures Statistics* (July 1966–67), 15 and *Commodity Futures Statistics* (July 1967–July 1968), 14.
4. Table 19 "Average annual midmonth and monthend long and short commitments of reporting and nonreporting traders," *Commodity Futures Statistics* (July 1957–July 1958), 68; Table 20 "Average annual midmonth and monthend long and short commitments of reporting and nonreporting traders," *Commodity Futures Statistics* (July 1967–Junly 1968), 52.
5. Table 16 "Contracts settled by delivery in each contract market, by future" *Commodity Futures Statistics* (July 1957–July 1958), 55; Table 19 "Contracts settled by delivery in each contract market, by future" *Commodity Futures Statistics,* (July 1968–July 1969), 49.
6. In re Volkart Brothers Inc., Volkart Brothers Company, Alfred Beodtker, and Kurt Muller, 20 Agriculture Decisions 306 (Commodity Exchange Authority, 1961), 317–318.
7. Ibid., 318.
8. Ibid.
9. Ibid., 318, 320.

10. Ibid., 318.
11. Ibid.
12. Ibid.
13. Ibid., 319.
14. Ibid., 319.
15. Ibid., 321.
16. Ibid., 324–325. These bales represented only a part of Volkart's global business. It had as of October 11 a total inventory of 112,675 bales of cotton and had commitments for the sale of 78,965 of these over the next 12 months, Ibid., 324.
17. Ibid., 312, 322–323. Prices at New Orleans, Houston and Galveston were about 0.3 cents a pound higher than the Memphis price.
18. Ibid., 320–321.
19. Ibid., 326.
20. *Major Transactions in the 1926 December Wheat Future*, Technical Paper 79, U.S. Department of Agriculture 20, 26, 46, 53–54.
21. In re Volkart, 331.
22. Ibid., 332.
23. Ibid., 333.
24. Ibid., 336.
25. Ibid., 338–339.
26. In re Volkart, 327.
27. Ibid., 341–342.
28. Volkart Brothers Inc. v Freeman, 311 F.2d 52 (Fifth Circuit U.S. Court of Appeals, 1962), 54–56.
29. Ibid., 58.
30. Based on the figures Rives cited, Volkart's average price on its New York futures was 35.25 cents for the 5.2 million pounds of cotton its 10,400 contracts represented and imputes a value for 5,000 bales of tendered cotton through that exchange. The New Orleans figure is based on the 35.38 cent floor, Volkart made sales at higher but undisclosed futures. With a normal futures to spot spread, Volkart would have received about $2,069,100. At the Memphis price, that much cotton would cost $1,984,400—though Volkart was buying more cotton at a different grade which suggested to Flavin that its futures operation was a speculation not a hedge.
31. Ibid., 57.

32. Volkart was the only long that received cotton through New York and New Orleans October futures: 5,100 bales to clear its October 15 open position, 300 bales on October 4. The October 4 deliveries would have brought the certificated total down to 4,963 on October 15. There is no evidence that any shorts defaulted. In re Volkart, 319.
33. Volkart Brothers v. Freeman, 59.
34. Ibid., 60.
35. Ibid.
36. This was the Exchange's point during the Commodity Exchange Authority proceeding, In re Volkart, 334; the Exchange reiterated this, as in Volkart v. Freeman, 57–58.
37. Volkart v. Freeman, 60.
38. In re Henner, 1264–1291.
39. In re Cargill Inc., 29 Agricultural Decisions 880, 914, cited In re Henner, 1280.
40. Cargill, Inc. v Hardin, 452 F.2d 1154 (Eighth Circuit U.S. Court of Appeals, 1971), 1159. The Commodity Exchange Authority's anxiety here was heightened over the eight years it took for its finding of manipulation to work its way through the courts where the Court of Appeals finally affirmed the finding.
41. In re Henner, 1158.
42. Ibid.
43. Cargill v Hardin, 1160–1161.
44. Ibid., 1161.
45. Ibid., 1169–1170.
46. Ibid., 1171.
47. Ibid., 1166–1167.
48. Cargill Inc., v Hardin, cert. denied, 406 U.S. 932 (U.S. Supreme Court, 1972) "One curious feature of the Commodity Exchange Act, and the regulations promulgated under the Act, is that 'manipulation' is referred to nearly 100 times without ever once being defined," as economists Robert W. Kolb and James A. Overdahl noted in a basic text on derivative instruments, adding: "Attempts to precisely define the term inevitably dissolve into circular logic: a manipulated price is an artificial price; an artificial price is one that has been manipulated." Robert W. Kolb and James A. Overdahl, *Futures, Options, and Swaps* (Malden, Mass.: Blackwell Publishing, 2007), 58.

49. In re Indiana Farm Bureau Cooperative Association and Louis M. Johnston, Docket 75-14, Opinion and Order, (Commodity Futures Trading Commission, 1982). Johnson cited Cargill v. Hardin, 452 F2d 1154, 1162 and a law review commentary on the Volkart decision: "The Delivery Requirement: An Illusory Bar to Regulation of Manipulation in Commodity Exchanges," Yale Law Journal, Volume 73 (1963), 171–186.

50. "The Vanishing Salad Oil, a $100 million mystery," New York Times, January 6, 1964, 97, 117.

51. H.R. 11788, Section 1(d) in *To Amend the Commodity Exchange Act, Hearings before the subcommittee on domestic marketing and consumer relations of the Committee on Agriculture on H.R. 11788* (Washington: Government Printing Office, 1966), 1.

52. Testimony of T.A. Hieronymus in *To Amend the Commodity Exchange Act, Hearings before the subcommittee ... on H.R. 11788*, 151.

53. Testimony of Harry Graham, To Amend the Commodity Exchange Act, Hearings before the subcommittee on domestic marketing and consumer relations of the Committee on Agriculture on H.R. 11,88 (Washington: Government Printing Office, 1966), 156.

54. Testimony of Harry Graham, To Amend the Commodity Exchange Act, Hearings before the subcommittee on domestic marketing and consumer relations of the Committee on Agriculture on H.R. 11788 (Washington: Government Printing Office, 1966), 156.

REFERENCES

Cargill, Inc. v Hardin, 452 F.2d 1154 (Eighth Circuit U.S. Court of Appeals, 1971) 1159

Cargill Inc., v Hardin, cert. denied, 406 U.S. 932 (U.S. Supreme Court, 1972)

Commodity Futures Statistics (July 1956–July 1957), (July 1957–July 1958), (July 1966–July 1967) and (July 1967–July 1968)

Great Western Food Distributors v Brannon 201 F 2nd 476 (U.S. Court of Appeals, 7th Circuit, 1953)

In re Cargill Inc., 29 Agricultural Decisions 880

In re David G Henner, 30 Agricultural Decisions 1151

In re Indiana Farm Bureau Cooperative Association and Louis M. Johnston, Docket 75-14 (Commodity Futures Trading Commission, 1982)

In re Volkart Brothers Inc., Volkart Brothers Company, Alfred Beodtker, and Kurt Muller, 20 Agriculture Decisions 306

Major Transactions in the 1926 December Wheat Future, Technical Paper 79, U.S. Department of Agriculture

"The Delivery Requirement: An Illusory Bar to Regulation of Manipulation in Commodity Exchanges," Yale Law Journal, Volume 73 (1963), 171–186

"The Vanishing Salad Oil, a $100 million mystery," New York Times, January 6, 1964, 97, 117

To Amend the Commodity Exchange Act, Hearings Before the Subcommittee on Domestic Marketing and Consumer Relations of the Committee on Agriculture on H.R. 11788 (Washington: Government Printing Office, 1966)

Volkart Brothers Inc. v Freeman, 311 F.2d 52 (Fifth Circuit U.S. Court of Appeals, 1962)

CHAPTER 7

The Mystery of Manipulation

Abstract Even as the case of the egg futures trading worked it way through the regulatory process, Henner and a partner launched another campaign to move futures prices, in this case, in the newer pork bellies futures market. This took the more traditional form of a market corner, In this case, regulators did not act, but many years later, the new Commodity Futures Trading Commission would suggest this was a mistake—even though, in another precedent-setting matter, the Indiana Farm Bureau manipulation case, they would formally reject the egg futures case argument that action proved intent and therefore manipulation to create a false price. The dissents in this case, however, highlighted a critical point: that financial market efficiency is not the same thing as the efficient allocation of resources and income.

Keywords Futures markets · Market manipulation · Artificial prices ·
Market corner · CFTC

For a few years after Henner's attempt to boost the November 1968 shell egg future, low-cost egg futures continued to attract speculators hoping to game the market, much as the infamous penny stocks of the period also would. At times, it could seem even to brokers in these markets as if gaming the suckers was the point; in the egg futures market, as if the real

D. Ress, *Market Manipulation and The Price of Eggs*,
https://doi.org/10.1007/978-3-031-87171-9_7

purpose of market had almost nothing at all to do with eggs. The egg business itself was less and less subject to the seasonal swings in production that drove traditional farm produce futures trading. Al Phillips, Jr. and twenty-three other traders, for instance, went to federal court to sue the Chicago Mercantile Exchange, certain of its officers and members of its Business Conduct Committee, alleging that they had monopolized trading in March 1970 fresh egg futures, causing the price to fall and forcing sales at artificially depressed market prices. Phillips' case had been joined to another federal lawsuit, this one involving a trader named Darryl Deaktor's complaint that he had lost $3,000 on two May 1970 frozen pork belly futures contracts, as a result of the Exchange's lack of action to prevent a manipulation by David Henner and a floor broker named Ann Cuneo. Henner was evidently not chastened by his wrist slap for the 1968 egg market game.[1] This time, though, Henner would try a more traditional tack: using a holding of real frozen pork bellies in a real warehouse to support futures market maneuvers, much as Gil Miller had with storage eggs in 1947.

With their pork bellies, however, Henner and Cuneo added a twist: much as a basketball or soccer player moving the ball and approaching an opponent might feint a move in one direction before darting off the other way, they used their physical holding to set the stage for a huge, one-day reversal of their large futures position. They were not the first to do this; one infamous case led Congress to ban futures trading in onions several years before, while Henner's egg futures trading, buying the board and then calling out his on-the-bell, limit-up bid were also a feint, though without benefit of a cash market position to enhance the signal. Yet while Judicial Officer Campbell concluded that the Henner had forced an artificial price by pushing the November future price up so sharply and so out of step with what was happening with the October and December futures, a new generation of regulators would find a different kind of feint that sparked even more dramatic one-day surge in corn futures in the summer of 1973—one that looked a lot more like the kind of squeeze that a dominant futures position and control of a large supply of a physical commodity—had not forced a false price and was not therefore an illegal manipulation. This had generated a July 20 price for the July corn future, formally a contract for delivery of corn by the end of the month, that was nearly fifty percent higher than what buyers were really paying that day delivery of real corn that month. Henner's egg trading, his maneuvers with Cuneo with pork bellies future and the 1973 corn futures squeeze all underscore how difficult regulators, law-makers and economists.

In Henner's maneuvers with the November 1968 shell egg future, U.S. Department of Agriculture Judicial Officer Donald Campbell had argued that the timing of Henner's moves demonstrated intent, necessary for a finding of a violation of law. In rebuttal, the economist L. Dee Belveal argued it was simply a mistake, a trade that was more like a reflex than anything intentional. The punishment Campbell imposed was mild, however, and Henner never bothered trying to test the ruling that he had manipulated the market. On the other hand. in the case of the pork bellies move, Henner and Cuneo's acquisition of real pork bellies and use of that holding to pressure the futures market were the kind of actions that regulators had long used to show intent in market manipulation. But in this case, regulators did not pursue a charge. Manipulation had never been formally defined in law, as the lobbying against efforts to do so led a discouraged Congress to give up, while trading in futures seemed more and more remote from real world commerce. Pork bellies—such a funny name, after all—seemed to epitomize this.

Pork bellies—the portions of slaughtered hogs that were destined to become bacon—were the basis of a new futures trading pit the Chicago Mercantile Exchange had set up as interest faded in its butter and egg futures. Like the shell egg futures Henner had traded in 1968, pork bellies offered a low-cost way to ride fast-moving price swings. The volume of trade in bellies was already by 1968 more than six times that in the egg pit. "It became apparent that members could not continue to subsist on eggs alone," exchange president Everette Harris would note some years later. While efforts to launch futures in scrap iron, frozen shrimp, frozen broiler chicken, hides and apples all failed, the Mercantile Exchange's pork belly futures did take off. The exchange marketed these as a way for meat packers to manage their risks for a commodity where supply peaked in the spring and fall and where demand also was somewhat seasonal, with a summer peak, apparently because of a seasonal public taste for bacon, lettuce and tomato sandwiches.[2]

Trading in pork bellies peaked in 1982, but as demand for bacon evened out through the year, the real interest in these futures was speculative. A fad for summertime bacon-lettuce-and-tomato sandwiches had generated the seasonal swing in cash prices that initially excited futures speculators, but bacon eventually became a common supplement to other dishes, as with, for instance, the bacon cheeseburgers that would become a fast food staple in the 1980s. Any need there might have been for a way to hedge against seasonal price swings faded, though in fact the industry that had boasted it found a use for every part of a hog except the squeal had a way to manage price risk with the Chicago Mercantile Exchange's live hog future. The name itself—pork bellies—suggested a disconnection from anything anyone produced or consumed. It was as if you did not really need to know anything about anything happening outside the trading pit. "The contract always had a mystery about it, and that accounts for its staying power," a later exchange chairman would comment. Pork bellies, like the exchange's other efforts to replace butter and eggs—live hogs, live beef cattle and Idaho potatoes—as well as its eventually-banned onion futures, all worked as futures because production was seasonal. However, bellies, which were frozen, could be stored for long enough periods to smooth out variations in actual supply. Storage, too, meant real bellies (or at least warehouse receipts for real bellies) like wheat, corn and soybeans, could be used in a futures market squeeze by bold enough operators.[3]

Henner and Cuneo held a large open position in the May 1970 pork bellies future, on the long side of the market. At the contract's expiry, they insisted on delivery of 346 car-lots (13.8 million pounds) of real bellies to close that position, though neither was in the business of turning bellies into bacon. That would have required a much larger commitment of funds than the financing Henner had had to arrange to support his move to stand for delivery—the bellies would have to go somewhere, after all. Even a paper transaction, buying warehouse receipts for already-stored bellies, would cost more than the tiny margin required for futures contract. Henner was able to finance his 198 car-lots through L.D. Schreiber & Company, the Mercantile Exchange member firm that also served as the clearing house for his trades. This would become a concern for the exchange since Schreiber, a clearing house, was supposed to be neutral actor responsible for ensuring integrity of the market. In this instance, however, the firm had taken sides with players who were evidently seeking to control supply to influence prices. In arranging this loan, Henner had demonstrated a clear intent for his market play: this was not a momentary reflex, as Dee Belveal had tried to suggest about Henner's 41.85 cent bid in the egg futures trading ring. Five of Cuneo's clients also took delivery, in their cases of another 61 cars, financing this, too, through Schreiber for $813,192. All in all she and Henner had control of 407 cars.[4]

Henner and Cuneo's long futures position and large holding of real pork bellies (actually, a holding of warehouse receipts) kept the May future's price high—high enough to prompt Deaktor's complaint that he had been caught in a squeeze, with two short contracts that he could clear only by paying an artificially high price. Since the two traders with the largest long position, Henner and Cuneo, were insisting on closing their contracts by taking delivery of real bellies rather than by trading futures, the effective supply of the long futures Deaktor needed to buy to close out his shorts was exceptionally tight. He had to bid what he argued was an artificially high price to do so: with bellies trading between 42 cents to 42.95 cents on the final day of trading, he would have paid between $3,360 to $3,436 to close out his shorts.[5] (For all his complaint that he lost $3,000, the closing price on expiry of the May pork belly futures was in fact down from earlier highs: the month before they were trading at about 43.40 cents, two months earlier, at 46 cents; Deaktor was complaining that the money he had to pay to close his shorts had wiped out his margin account.)[6]

Nobody else complained. Nevertheless, as the May pork bellies contract expired, exchange president Everette Harris approached L.D. Schreiber to say he was worried a major manipulation was in the works. His concern, however, was not with the May future. Henner and Cuneo's insistence on physical delivery to clear their long position, may have looked to Deaktor like an intentional effort in a well-tried manner to squeeze shorts and force him to pay a manipulated and unfairly high price, but his loss was too small-time to worry the exchange. Instead, Harris thought Henner and Cuneo were planning some other, larger manipulation, though it was not clear exactly what.

There were at least two ways that would have moved prices in opposite directions, he felt. One possibility, Harris said, involved the dramatic price signaling from a large open position. "Here's what these people [Henner and Cuneo] are shooting at. They're going to take delivery of these bellies, 400 cars in May, and they're going one of two ways ... in either July or August they were going to withhold these bellies from sale, then go short ... and deliver the 400 cars and break the market to their own profit," Harris recalled telling Schreiber. The other was that Henner and Cuneo planned to sell their bellies, at whatever price they could get in July, to create a shortage while they took a large, long position in the July or August contract to create a squeeze. Schreiber told Harris not to worry, "because we are in charge of this situation," promising that "we would protect the fair and good name of the Exchange." Schreiber also assured Harris that if he saw tightness in the futures market, he would order Henner and Cuneo to deliver their actual bellies in the futures market.

Henner and Cuneo opted for something different: a dramatic, one day switch in their position. They started with moves like the ones Harris outlined in his second scenario. Between May 27 and July 17, 1970, Henner and Cuneo sold 164 car-lots of their bellies, mostly without the inspection certificates that could have allowed them to be used to clear July or August futures. Selling them depressed cash prices and led speculators in futures to expect a drop in the July contract. The two took an additional step that Harris did not foresee. Henner and Cuneo fed this sentiment by building up a huge, short position in the July future, one that would eventually amount to 329 contracts. The price of the July future over this period fell from about 41 cents before they began this maneuver to stabilize around 38 cents. On July 14, the Exchange's Business Conduct Committee asked Henner and Cuneo what they were doing by selling off their holdings of real pork bellies (or warehouse receipts) without inspection—in effect, putting the bellies out of reach of anyone seeking to unwind a short, including themselves as the largest shorts. It seemed to make no sense to the committee, but Henner and Cuneo reportedly managed to satisfy any concerns that they might be planning to squeeze traders with long open positions. The committee, which had shrugged off Deaktor's complaint, took no action on a complaint that Schreiber had violated its rules when financing the purchases in the first place.[7]

Henner and Cuneo made their moves on Monday, July 20, 1970, four days before the July contract expired. Here, as with Henner's egg market moves, timing mattered. The date was close enough to the contract expiry to make the question of clearing an open position ever more urgent, while acting on the expiry date or the day before could have almost certainly triggered a manipulation charge, or, worse, a default with traders unable to clear positions. That would have been the kind of failure of the market that would scare off players for years to come.

On July 20, then, Henner sold the rest of his car-lots of bellies, 120 in all, pushing the future price still lower. He and Cuneo then began to quickly unwind their 329-contract short position, with long contracts at lower prices—and then, kept buying, ending the day with a combined long position of 261 contracts. In one frenzied day of trading, they bought 590 long contracts The price of the July future spiked—trading well above cash price for bellies, depressed as it was by Henner's sales, at a time when in theory the futures and cash price should have converged. Henner and Cuneo's careful timing won them profits both from clearing their initial short position, while the price spike they led, which saw future rise from 39.40 cents to 40.70 cents, allowed them to unwind their long position at prices near the day's high.[8]

Henner and Cuneo's maneuvering in the pork bellies market was the mirror image of an earlier manipulation in another futures market that the Chicago Mercantile Exchange hoped would replace its shrinking butter and egg business: onions. Onions, like shell eggs, spoiled quickly. Supply was extremely seasonal, as shell eggs had been before some of the new production practices that had wrongfooted Henner in 1968. Both characteristics were why two speculators, Sam Siegel and Vincent Kosuga, were able to play that low-cost market as it grew in the 1950s. Much as Henner and Cuneo would do, Siegel and Kosuga aimed to make a profit with a dramatic change in their open position in onion futures while withholding and then releasing a large supply of real onions to enhance pressure on the futures price. Their first move was to send the price of November 1955 onion futures soaring. Kosuga, a New York onion shipper, bought a 928 car-lot long position, pushing prices higher as shorts covered their position. With these proceeds, they then assembled a more than 1,000 car-lot, 30-million-pound inventory of actual onions—about 98% of the deliverable supply for anyone seeking to close a short position with onions (or warehouse receipts for actual bags of onions) instead of a countervailing long.[9] This manipulation eventually led Congress to ban futures trading in onions: the only farm product so barred from futures trading.[10]

Something like the long to short switch that Kosuga plotted to push up the price of the November 1955 and send the March 1956 future's price plunging, was what Chicago Mercantile Exchange president Harris thought Henner had in mind. When he learned that Henner had sold the 120 car-lots of pork bellies to meat packers, so that they were unavailable if any traders opted to stand for delivery to close open positions, Harris grew even more worried. He was so concerned that when on the morning of July 21, the day after the July pork belly future expired, he called Donald L. Tendick, then the Acting Regional Director of the Commodity Exchange Authority, to call his attention to the squeeze he feared was coming. Tendick said there was no need for the Authority to act. That day, Harris also visited Schreiber to discuss the liquidation of the July pork bellies contract, saying he was "worried about a little tightness in the market, and he thought he would like it to be loosened up." Schreiber said he did not feel there was a problem but suggested that Harris speak directly to Cuneo. Harris then called Cuneo, who agreed to liquidate her futures position, but said that since she expected to profit from the sale of the actual pork bellies she owned and refused to make them available for delivery on the futures market.[11]

Challenged by the Board of Governors about his trading in the July futures and his handling of the pork deliveries delivered against his May long contracts, Henner pleaded guilty to violating an exchange rule that said traders could not finance their speculative positions with a clearing house, like Schreiber. The board fined Henner $10,000 and suspended his right to trade on the floor for two years; Schreiber pleaded no contest. The board found Cuneo guilty of violating the same rules. A Commodity Exchange Authority investigation continued for another nine months, but eventually concluded there was not enough evidence to bring a charge of manipulation.

A later review of the exchange's handling of the affair by the Authority's successor, the Commodity Futures Trading Commission, concluded in 1979—that is, nine years later—that the series of acts by Henner and Cuneo "strongly support the conclusion that said market was manipulated."[12] But although the Commission, like the Authority before it, had always said preventing manipulation was an essential mission task both for the exchanges' internal self-regulation and for government regulators, it took no further action against Henner and Cuneo. "[W]e are particularly mindful that our predecessor agency, which was apprised and consulted during the development of the alleged manipulation and which investigated the incidents immediately after they occurred, saw neither non-feasance on the CME's [Chicago Mercantile Exchange's] part nor reason to take administrative action against either the exchange or the alleged manipulators," the Commodity Futures Trading Commission, wrote, after reviewing the matter. "Nine years after the fact, we are disinclined to second-guess our predecessor on these points. However, we do wish to caution against future reference to or reliance upon the regulatory policies of our predecessor agency should such a situation as arose here occur in the future."[13] As for whether the exchange did a sufficiently effective job policing trading, the Commission essentially shrugged its shoulders and commented that "Even the most diligent and vigorous self-regulatory efforts may not lead to the detection and prevention of a manipulation."[14]

When the new commission, empowered by a 1974 law that still did not include a definition of manipulation, asked about the largest one-day spike in the price of a futures contract, the definition that Campbell had relied upon in the egg futures case no longer seemed to provide much clarity. Considering the largest ever one-day rise in a futures contract price, the new commission would look at Campbell's Henner ruling, and decide that seeking the highest price possible—as Henner had with the limit-up 41.85 cent bid that Marlowe King hit—was not enough to prove the intention necessary to violate a law, especially a law that did not bother to define manipulation of a market.

Seeking the highest price possible was what the Indiana Farm Bureau Cooperative Association and Louis M. Johnston, manager of the cooperative's grain division did on July 20 1973, as the Chicago Board of Trade July corn future expired. It had been a challenging summer for the corn trade—the actual buying and selling of real corn, that is—for during that time exports had surged, including to the Soviet Union. These big export moves meant shortages of rail cars and elevators to move and store the 1973 harvest in Iowa, Illinois and Indiana, including delivery to the July future's designated delivery points. There were problems with the quality of harvested corn in some areas, as well. Of a harvest estimated at 12.1 million bushels within easy delivery of Chicago, only 4.5 million bushels were said to meet the Board of Trade contract's specifications, while the Commodity Futures Trading Commission's Division of Enforcement said a closer look showed the amount was really just 511,000 bushels.[15] There was nowhere near enough corn to clear the 17 million bushel open position as of July 19, the day before the July future expired, the Board of Trade's directors realized; shorts would have no real alternative but to cover their positions with futures and the exchange's ten-cent daily limit on price movements meant the market might not be able to cope. The directors voted to remove the limit for the final day's trading.[16]

On July 20, then, the price of the future jumped from its July 19 closing price of $2.59-1/2 a bushel, rising by about 40 cents in increasingly frantic trading that morning to just under $3.00, the point at which Johnston secretly told the Farm Bureau's broker he aimed to sell the cooperative's open position, after publicly declaring that morning the cooperative planned to stand for delivery on some 2,010,000 of its 4,705,000-bushels-worth of long July futures—far more corn than was at hand, and so ramping up the pressure on shorts to bid up the price of the future.[17]

In any event, prices rose nearly but not quite to the point where Johnston could sell futures for the more than $3.00 per bushel price he was hoping for. Seeing this, at 10 a.m. Johnston narrowed his combined buy-sell spread orders, bringing the implied price for the July future to $3.00-1/2. He also put in a straight sell order for 150,000 bushels of the July future at $3.00. Both were still well ahead of the market at that point, despite the pressure of the Farm Bureau's standing for delivery declaration. The spread order was only completed nearly ninety minutes later at 11.26 a.m., two minutes after the July future touched $3.00. Shortly after 11:30 a.m., with 30 minutes to go before trading ended and the July future expired, the broker telephoned Johnston to report a peculiar situation in the pit: after the surge up to $3.00, nobody was offering any futures for sale and liquidation of the still enormous open position was faltering. At this point, Johnston gave the Farm Bureau's broker instructions to sell a total of 490,000 bushels at stepped-up prices of $3.70, $3.75, $3.80, $3.85 and $3.90. This was the signal that panicked traders. They stampeded, scrambling to buy whatever they could, sending the price skyrocketing. The five orders were executed beginning at 11:38 a.m. July corn quickly reached a high of $3.90, and at the closing bell only five thousand bushels of Johnston's order at $3.90 remained unsold.[18]

The Farm Bureau had a large long position, one of three such traders, but with less than thirty percent of open interest in the July future at the start of the day; there was one short with nearly as large a position as the Farm Bureau, and its (very junior) trader's moves now seem to have exacerbated the surge in the July future's price in the final twenty minutes of trading. Sumitomo Shoji America's four-million-bushel short position "seems to have been a gamble on the government's rumored announcement of new export controls," CFTC Commissioner James Stone concluded. This was, he noted, "reckless behavior ... an unusually compelling example of an exogenous influence on price movements," for Sumitomo's trader then chased after the Farm Bureau's stepped price orders as they drove the July future ever higher to its $3.90 a bushel peak. "It may remain forever a mystery why" the Sumitomo trader did that, said the commission's chairman, Philip McBride Johnson. "The hazy record on this subject suggests, however, that Sumitomo's large short position may have been placed by a company subordinate without authority from his superiors," Johnson noted. "If so, the subordinate may have been reluctant to highlight his actions by making large purchases of cash corn for the company's account at that time."[19] Here, perhaps, the Sumitomo trader was demonstrating one of the "risks of various kinds," which along with real world transactions costs, finite capital, and other limits to arbitrage, would lead financial economist Stephen Figlewski to suggest that the law of one price might not always apply in derivative markets, since it assumed cost- and risk-less arbitrage, leaving open the possible of false pricing signals.[20]

Farm Bureau director Johnston testified that he placed his stepped-up sell orders to help the market liquidate. But he moved well after other longs had. By the time his broker told the pit the cooperative was selling, most other longs had closed their position: the Farm Bureau's long contracts at this point had grown from thirty percent of the total long position to more than sixty percent. Johnston's tactic at this point, too, "does not address the issue of price," commissioner Stone noted. "With 30 years of experience in both futures and cash trading, Johnston surely knew that orders priced closer to the cash market would be at least as useful in helping the liquidation." Johnston would have been "fully cognizant of the pressure the situation imposed on the shorts and their presumed desire to avoid a default. ... It was too late for the shorts to safely acquire cash corn" since nobody could tell if prices around $3.00, which still would have been more than $1.00 a bushel above the cash price, would be enough to move enough corn of the right quality to Chicago in time.[21]

In the corn pit at the Board of Trade at 11:30 a.m. on July 20, 1973, with a half hour to go before a short without corn in hand would have to strike a deal, there was precisely the eyeball to eyeball confrontation that Belveal had proposed but that had not in fact existed when Henner called out his 41.85 cent bid for the November egg future. In the corn futures pit, shorts were in a desperate position; in the egg futures pit, they had mostly been confused and then angered by what clearly seemed to have been an effort to "bull the market" (as the floor broker Arthur Parz had described Henner's trading.) On the floor of the Board of Trade, in contrast, "The shorts were effectively signaling their weakness by frantically bidding up the price," Stone noted. "It is hard to see step-up orders under these conditions as not having a purpose to dictate an upward price or price trend or, alternatively, to force default. The latter, Johnston agreed, he did not expect."[22]

Moreover, Stone noted, Johnston would have known the price was artificially high, since at the same time, the cooperative was busily shopping for immediately deliverable corn to fill its large export orders—orders for more corn than its members were on track to harvest. It bid $2.42 for Chicago cash corn of deliverable quality on July 19, and $2.65 for cash corn on July 20, even as it was selling the July future at $3.70 to $3.90 a bushel. On the following Monday, it closed a deal for 360,000 bushels at $2.67 a bushel.[23] Two other major corn merchants—Cargill and Continental Grain—were bidding less than $2.67 a bushel for immediate delivery of real corn in Chicago that day, while the U.S. Department of Agriculture's price support operation, the Agriculture Stabilization and Conservation Service, quoted Chicago cash corn on that date only slightly higher, at $2.70-3/8. No buyer in the cash market paid more than $2.91 per bushel for corn for the rest of July, while CPC International, Inc., another major merchant firm, acquired 600,000 bushels of delivery grade corn at Chicago on July 31, 1973 at $2.78 per bushel (traders with short positions in the July future had until July 31 to deliver corn if they chose to close their positions that way.) "The quantity purchased by CPC approximated the average daily amount that Sumitomo would have had to acquire between July 20 and the end of the month if it had chosen to make delivery on its entire short futures position," commission chairman Johnson noted. "While not conclusive on the issue, this evidence suggests that the cash market was capable of handling transactions of this magnitude at prices well below the July 20 futures price," he wrote, adding: "Here, the deviation of roughly $1.20, or 30%, cannot be fully explained by any possible uncertainty over the true value of cash corn."[24]

Was $3.90 a bushel, then, an artificial price? "The tight corn supply and Indiana Farm's standing for delivery were legitimate forces of supply and demand which caused futures prices to rise," the commission majority ruled. "Standing for delivery as they did was [the cooperative's] contractual right and was motivated by pre-existing commercial needs," the majority noted.[25] The problem was on the other side of the market that day, for "The panic bidding of shorts who were totally unprepared to deliver caused the most dramatic spurt in prices."[26] They had guessed wrong about a U.S. Department of Agriculture response to that summer's disappointing harvest, expecting that the government would impose export controls on corn similar to those it had put on soybeans. "When that possibility was removed after the close on July 18, shorts in no position to fulfill their delivery obligations bid the price up the limit on July 19 and beyond on July 20," the majority noted. "While the resultant $1.20 price rise was the largest one day price rise ever recorded for corn, it must be remembered that the daily price limit had been removed allowing for such an unprecedented rise"—that is, that Board of Trade directors decided on a completely unregulated, free market approach to find the price to balance supply and demand.[27] In this situation, as with the Volkart decision, the commission majority argued that it was up to actors on the other side of the market to have looked out for themselves: "We also note in this regard the irresponsible market behavior of the shorts here," their opinion noted; as in the Volkart case "we find that it is irresponsible market behavior for shorts to enter the delivery month, especially where low cash supplies are evident, without making adequate delivery preparations."[28]

There was in this analysis a peculiar disconnection between the dealing in the market for real corn(and the futures market, the majority seemed to be saying, so that "Against the backdrop of an inert cash market, comparison of the futures price and nominal cash quotations is of little value in assessing the true economic value of corn in Chicago on July 20." On the one hand, the supply of real, actual corn was tight because of a disappointing harvest and large export shipments—so tight, that in the futures market, the cooperative opted to stand for delivery, to insist on getting real corn to clear roughly half of its open position. On the other, as the majority put it, the cash market for corn was inert—even though major commercial operators, including the cooperative, were buying corn for immediate delivery through this period, and in large amounts. "Thus, given the unique market and economic forces of supply and demand operating on the July 1973 corn futures contract, while the prices reached on July 20 were high ...based upon market factors we have noted, we conclude that the price trend on July 20 was indeed reflective of the legitimate forces of supply and demand," the majority concluded.[29]

There was no artificial price on July 20, the majority ruled, because Johnston was simply seeking the best price. Moreover, the majority held when it declared that $3.90 a bushel was a real price for the July future that the integrity of the market was at stake. The majority commissioners insisted on the point that Judge Rives made in the Volkart case that the issue was that shorts (Sumitomo's junior trader in this case) had contracts to fulfil. At the same time, a holder of open long positions "if dissatisfied that the price bid or offered ...- can make or force delivery of the actual product," the majority wrote. All the Sumitomo Shoji trader needed to do, that is, was to go out and find 4 million bushels of corn.[30] The price was real, the free market was right, and its rules had to be followed. Legitimate demand and supply forces had played out.

The problem, Commissioner Stone wrote in reply, was that "The concept of relative legitimacy in supply and demand forces takes one quickly beyond economics ...it apparently rests on a value judgment to be made after the fact." Implied, moreover, was a second value judgement, that market equilibrium is efficient, at least in the usual economic sense—that is, in the allocation of goods and services, of resources and production, or of returns on capital, land and labor, Stone wrote. The reason this is a problem, he continued, is because efficiency in a financial market is not the same thing as economic efficiency. Economic efficiency, Stone said, is a goal rather than a provable accomplishment (since the theory that free market prices generate the most efficient distributions cannot be tested by experiment). "A financial market is called efficient to the extent that its prices are those which would prevail if every investor had possession of all relevant market information," Stone noted.[31] A false rumor, as with Campbell's half-analogy between a false rumor and Henner's 41.85 cent bid for the November future,[32] would make a financial market operate less efficiently in this sense, Stone noted. "[B]ut it would be drawn toward financial efficiency by any scoundrel who, having arranged the fire bombing of his competitor's grain storage, placed his orders long to enjoy the impending shortage."[33] Efficiency in this financial market sense, is concerned only with the distribution of information and not to its content: that everyone concerned could see Henner's buying the board and his still-higher, final 41.85 cent bid, as Belveal would argue, not on what it meant. In this view of efficiency nobody cared, or should, about what Henner's moves had to do with the price of eggs.

But they should. For if you could say, as the majority had, that some factors in a cash market, such as the availability of corn at prices less than $3 a bushel, were not legitimate while factors unique to a futures market were—the perplexing behavior of a junior trader at Sumitomo Shoji or Henner's moves in the egg futures pit—than the idea that futures serve a price discovery and hedging function becomes nonsense. That—as in Henner's egg market moves—willing buy and seller did strike their deals posed a fundamental question about the theory of pricing. As Johnson put it: "if all influences in the futures market are absorbed into the supply demand equation, it would follow logically and almost automatically that no futures price could be considered artificial."[34]

NOTES

1. Chicago Mercantile Exchange v Deaktor 414 US 113 (U.S. Supreme Court, 1973). The Supreme Court ruled that the dispute should have gone to the Commodity Exchange Authority, but Phillips never pursued this, suggesting a lack of faith in the regulator's enforcement efforts.
2. Everette B. Harris, *History of the Chicago Mercantile Exchange*, https://legacy.farmdoc.illinois.edu/irwin/archive/books/Futrs_Tradng_in_Livestck/Futures_Trading_in_%20Livestock_Part%20I_2.pd.
3. Ibid.; Joe Castaldo, "Commodities," *Canadian Business*; August 2011: 11.
4. In the Matter of the Chicago Mercantile Exchange, Commodity Futures Trading Commission Docket 75-8 Opinion of the Commission, 2.
5. "Prices of Commodity Futures," *New York Times*, May 21, 1970, 57.
6. Ibid., April 21, 1970, 57; March 21, 1970.
7. In the Matter of the Chicago Mercantile Exchange, 2; Prices from the *New York Times* daily commodity market price reports, May 15 to July 21.
8. In the Matter of the Chicago Mercantile Exchange, 2; "Listing of Prices of Commodity Futures," *New York Times*, July 21, 1970, 44.
9. In re: Vincent W Kosuga, Sam S. Siegel, and National Produce Distributors, Inc., Commodity Exchange Authority Docket 73, (1956) Complaint: 3–4.
10. The Onion Futures Act, 7 USC § 13-1.
11. In the Matter of the Chicago Mercantile Exchange, 2–3.
12. Ibid., 5.
13. Ibid.
14. Ibid., 6.

15. In re Indiana Farm Bureau Cooperative Association and Louis M. Johnston, Docket 75-14, Opinion and Order (Commodity Futures Trading Commission, 1982), 2 2, https://www.cftc. gov/sites/default/files/idc/groups/public/@lrceacases/docume nts/ceacases/indiana-johnston-dec1982-9.pdf (The opinion and order is also found at Commodity Futures Law Reporter (CCH) 21796).
16. Ibid., 2, 42.
17. Ibid., 43.
18. Ibid., 2, 34, 43, 44.
19. Ibid., 18, note 6.
20. Stephen Figlewski "Derivatives Valuation Based on Arbitrage: The Trade is Crucial," *The Journal of Futures Markets*, Vol. 37, No. 4, (2017), 316–327.
21. In re Indiana Farm Bureau, 43.
22. Ibid., 3.
23. Ibid.
24. Ibid., 19.
25. Ibid., 12.
26. Ibid., 13.
27. Ibid.
28. Ibid., 12.
29. Ibid.
30. Ibid, 10.
31. Ibid., 31. For this view of financial market efficiency, see, e.g. Eugene F. Fama, "Efficient Capital Markets: A Review of Theory and Empirical Work," *Journal of Finance*, Vol. 25, No. 2 (May 1970), 383–417; Sanford J. Grossman and Joseph Stiglitz, "Information and Competitive Price Systems," *American Economic Review*. Vol. 66, No. 2 (May 1976), 246–53; Robert Verrecchia, "Consensus Beliefs, Information Acquisition, and Market Information Efficiency," *American Economic Review*, Vol. 70, No. 5 (December 1980), 874–884.
32. In re Henner, 1234.
33. In re Indiana Farm Bureau, 31.
34. Ibid., 18, note 8.

CHAPTER 8

Conclusion: Banging the Close

Abstract Henner's close-of-trading drama in the egg futures market would become a not uncommon way of generating a artificial price in derivatives trading, particularly in derivatives with underlying assets that were also derivatives. While the Commodity Futures Trading Commission was able to sustain manipulation cases in some of these situations (in electricity and natural gas futures) it failed in a case involving interest rate futures in a decision that essentially held there was no such thing as an artificial price as long as both sides of a deal knew, or thought they knew, what they were doing. The point here: the dynamics of a competitive derivative market primarily functioning for price discovery, whether in egg futures or interest rates, can force prices to a trader's predetermined goals that have nothing to do with the price of an underlying asset.

Keywords Futures market · Artificial prices · Market manipulation · Derivatives

In 1975, with the start of the Commodity Futures Trading Commission's re-examination of David Henner and Ann Cuneo's pork bellies play, Henner decided it was time to retire. Then in his mid-40s, he had been doing well with other business interests including a nightclub in the once sleepy Jamaican resort town of Montego Bay just as its Tryall and Round

D. Ress, *Market Manipulation and The Price of Eggs*, https://doi.org/10.1007/978-3-031-87171-9_8

Hill resorts opened for business in the 1960s. Despite paying a $10,000 fine to the exchange as a kind of apology for crossing the line of what even the Chicago Mercantile Exchange directors considered fair dealing in pork bellies, he had the funds—and yacht—available to make possible his decision to sail around the world, setting off from Newport, Rhode Island, and finishing fourteen years later, in 1989, in New Zealand.[1] But "banging the close," as Henner's egg futures tactic came to known, did not stop after his brief suspension for his egg futures market move.

In the years since Henner made his egg market move and gamed what was then the new and fast-growing market in the even more volatile pork bellies future, new derivatives contracts in intangible assets: interest rates and electricity flows, for instance, and derivatives on derivatives including options on U.S. Treasury bond futures and futures contracts on interest rate swaps. Trading volumes expanded exponentially. More speculators, especially large institutions including investment banks and hedge funds flocked to futures, options and swaps markets. When the underlying asset of a derivative was not something you could hold—a fresh egg, a handful of corn, some bacon—but merely an idea, like the derivative instrument itself, it was easier to assume cost-less and risk-less arbitrage between asset and derivative. More actors, more liquidity and a belief that transaction costs could be ignored brought markets in new-style derivatives even closer to the mathematically perfect machinery of theory. Yet the machinery of these near-perfect markets still spit out artificial prices. Even in multi-billion dollar market movements, shows that the individual still mattered.

At the 7:30 a.m. opening of trading on October 22 1992 in the U.S. Treasury bond future on the Chicago Board of Trade, Darryl Zimmerman and his friend Anthony Catalfo began selling, building a $3.2 billion short position in a frenzied half hour while at the same time snapping up every one of some 25,000 available put options on the future (options to sell the T-bond future). The bond futures plunged; traders read the heavy selling of the future and the heavy buy of put options as a signal of ... nobody was quite sure, since the critical market-moving report about unemployment report was still ten minutes away.[2] "I did in the bond pit what every trader dreams about," Zimmerman said much later, after floor brokers and clerks from the clearing house holding his $50,000 insufficient funds check for his margin payments dragged him out of the T-bond pit. "You spend half of every day thinking about what would happen if you could trade large enough to move a market by yourself, to play like the big firms and banks do. I had everyone in the pit coming to me. I was the market. The exchanges just don't want to admit the market can be controlled by one guy, especially by someone like me, but I proved it can. Almost."[3]

Banging the close was a way to have that control. It worked especially well for firms that traded derivatives and derivatives on those derivatives, as the Spokane, Washington energy firm, Avista Energy did with New York Mercantile Exchange futures on month-end delivery of electricity in California as well as swaps based on daily electricity deliveries. The swaps paid or required payment based on the difference between any one day's wholesale price for power at and the daily settlement price for the futures.[4] The key to whether Avista would be paid or would pay for any of these swaps was based instead on the weighted average of trades completed in the final two minutes of trading of those futures—for the PV future, which was based on delivery at the Palo Verde power plant in Arizona, this occurred between 3:23 p.m. and 3:25 p.m. New York time and for the COB future, based on the metered flow of electrons on a wire crossing the California-Oregon state line, between 3:28 p.m. and 3:30 p.m.

Those two, two-minute periods looked like an opportunity to Avista vice president for risk management William Taylor. He sounded out a New York Mercantile Exchange member, Anthony J. DiPlacido, whose trading badge JADE gave him access to the floor, with his proposal to flood the market during the settlement period. The two men launched the scheme at about 3:20 p.m. on April 24 1998, the last day to trade the May future, when Taylor called DiPlacido with an order to sell 50 May futures—and to "sell them down as hard as we can during the close." "What's my limit down to?" DiPlacido asked. "As low as possible … we are trying to get a settlement," Taylor said. Seconds later, Taylor called in an order to sell another ten futures, telling DiPlacido's floor clerk to pass the word that he wanted these sales "at market worst"—that is, as low as possible. After doing that, in this case by hitting all the bids to buy electricity and then offering to sell futures at levels even lower, DiPlacido sold 65 PV futures contracts for Avista during the critical two minutes at progressively lower prices. Afterward, DiPlacido told his clerk not to use the word "worst" when relaying a customer's order since that could get him into trouble with the exchange's market surveillance officers; instead, he suggested, say "don't be shy." DiPlacido also told the clerk that Avista wanted to trade in this way because of its open position in over-the-counter options; a lower futures price would make the firm's options with their low execution triggers more valuable.[5]

A month later, in the final two minutes of trading in the June PV future, with an order from Avista to sell these at market worst, DiPlacido sold 150 futures: afterward, he telephoned Taylor and boasted that he had been like aircraft carrier entering New York harbor while the other traders in the ring were like sailboats trying to cross as he went by: "whatever bid they gave me, cause they were bidding for three's and two's, I offered right through them … I said 'sold,' 'at 20,' they gave me a 40 bid, 'at 20,' what do you guys want, so that made it very simple." The settlement price for June was down 53 cents from the average of the hour before those last two minutes; this too boosted the value of Avista's options position.[6]

Avista switched its stance for the August futures, when Robert Kristufek, a trader on the firm's energy desk in Houston (some 2,100 miles south and east of the company's actual Washington State business of producing and distributing electricity) called DiPlacido's clerk on the morning of July 27 to tell him to expect another big order. The clerk said he might need two floor brokers to handle that much business; as DiPlacido explained in a follow-up call, doing that would make Avista's move "a lot more believable if he walks in there first … the whole ring will think he knows something." Later that day, at about 3:20 pm, Kristufek called DiPlacido's clerk with the instruction that he wanted to settlement price to "go to the moon," and gave an order for 250 PV futures. Staying on the phone through the two minutes that would determine the settlement price, Kristufek told the clerk he wanted an "ugly close," which the clerk understood to mean buying contracts at increasingly higher prices.[7]

Standing immediately behind DiPlacido on the floor, the clerk said he saw DiPlacido violate brokers' offers to sell futures by bidding to buy futures at still higher prices—that is, that DiPlacido was confounding the expectation that a buyer wants to pay the lowest possible price. Other traders, meanwhile, stepped over to complain to the clerk about the way DiPlacido had traded, by bidding through their offers. Mercantile Exchange member John McCann testified that he observed DiPlacido bidding to buy the PV future at $58 when another broker, with badge NNJA, was offering to sell at $57. After the close, exchange member Brian Caesar, who had handled Avista orders in the past, phoned Kristufek to say he had bid $55.10 for two futures when "all of a sudden, JADE went 55, 56, 56 bid, 57 bid, 58 bid." Altogether, DiPlacido bought 207 futures for Avista in those final two minutes; but shortly after 3:25 p.m. Kristufek called to say they had not bought enough: Surprised, DiPlacido asked "what do you mean you needed them all?" which his clerk believed meant that DiPlacido thought it had been sufficient to move the settlement.[8]

Kristufek brushed off DiPlacido's suggestion that he could buy more PV futures in after-the-close dealing; and within seconds was on the phone again, to the clerk, with an order for 150 August COB futures and an instruction that he wanted the COB Close to be "ugly." Other traders kept coming up to the clerk to complain about DiPlacido's trading; McCann later testified he saw DiPlacido bidding above other traders' offer prices to sell the future while exchange member Anthony Birbilis testified that while he was offering to sell at $45.50, DiPlacido was bidding $46. That day, the PV future settlement price jumped by more than five percent; the next day, the PV future fell 9.5%. The COB future settled 7.75% higher; it fell 10.5% the next day.[9]

For the Commodity Futures Trading Commission, this was the first time it considered a manipulation case based on trading floor practices in an adjudicated decision. All of the CFTC's manipulation cases since taking over regulation of futures market in 1974, under a law that still did not define manipulation, were based on market corners or squeezes; DiPlacido's case was the first since Henner to turn on bidding practice. In the Henner case, as summarized in the CFTC opinion on DiPlacido's trading:

> the Judicial Officer, whose decision was the final decision of the agency, concluded that Henner, through his trading activity on the trading floor of the Chicago Mercantile Exchange, "paid more than he had to ... for the purpose of causing the closing price to be at [a] high level," and on that basis found Henner liable for manipulation.[10]

The commission fined DiPlacido $1 million, doubling the penalty its administrative law judge had recommended and that DiPlacido has protested was excessive. The U.S. Court of Appeals for the Second Circuit was unconvinced by DiPlacido's efforts to overturn the decision by claiming that the commission had pursued the case in a biased manner and that it was trying to punish him for commonplace trading practices. It was a major victory for the commission. The court, also citing Judicial

Officer Campbell's opinion about Henner's egg futures trades, confirmed the commission decision and the $1 million fine: an artificial price could rise simply from considering when a trader acted and when he or she did not.[11]

The CFTC levied a larger, $7.5 million fine on Amaranth Advisors for a similar move to generate swap payments by flooding a futures market, this time in natural gas, with the sale of thousands of futures during the thirty-minute settlement period for the gas future on the New York Mercantile Exchange. Brian Hunter, Amaranth's trading desk manager, had launched the scheme with a text message to one of his traders "Sweet Friday". "Pain everywhere," the trader replied. "Just need H [the March gas future] to get smashed on settle then day is done" Hunter messaged back. Some 21 seconds after the settlement period ended, with the formal report of a sharply lower settlement that would mean a large payment on Amaranth's 12,000 swaps, a triumphant Hunter messaged the desk: "I am flexing here."[12] Hunter and the Amaranth trades used the same tactic with May and August futures that year.

With the DiPlacido and Amaranth decisions, the CFTC seemed at last to be able to prove a market price was artificial, the key to making a case for market manipulation. But a federal appeals court judge's ruling when the commission tried again to market this case would overturn those findings. The judge, in the case of Donald Wilson and DRW Investments, essentially held that a market price was always right. Judge Richard Sullivan's ruling on DRW's thousands of bids for futures on interest rate swaps in effect said there was no such thing as an artificial price in a derivatives market as long as there were parties willing to buy and sell—even if they did not strike a deal.[13]

This glance into the price discovery function of derivatives markets started during the Groundhog Day blizzard of 2011, with its heavy snowfall—21 inches in Chicago—and roaring winds paralyzed traffic and caused power blackouts from Texas to Nova Scotia, DRW Investments' bids, posted electronically for futures on 10-year interest rate swaps attracted the attention of New York-based MF Global, an investment bank. As the storm raged outside DRW's Chicago offices, without yet reaching New York, a DRW broker told MF's trader that he could buy up to $1 billion worth; in the end they struck a deal for $250 million. The price, expressed as an interest rate, was 16/100ths of a percentage point above the closing rate on 10-year swaps in the over-the-counter market.[14]

"As it turned out, the deal cratered," Judge Richard Sullivan of the U.S. Court of Appeals for the Second Circuit later recounted. When DRW and MF submitted the deal to the International Derivatives Clearing House, it was unable to process the transaction because of the power outages caused by the storm, and when DRW's founder, Donald Wilson, tried to clear the deal the following day, MF Global backed out.[15] "Wilson was livid; he demanded an explanation and endeavored to have the exchange compel MF Global to live up to its end of the bargain," Sullivan wrote. It was a big deal for DRW, and when Wilson asked the International Derivatives Clearinghouse to step in, the clearing house took the opportunity to ask about complaints other firms had filed about DRW's trading.[16]

DRW was an active bidder in the market for futures contracts on interest rate swaps—derivatives of derivatives. These were futures contracts on exchanges of cash arranged in the over-the-counter market for actual interest rate swaps; these, in turn, were derivative contracts promising payments based on the difference between the yield a holder of debt securities—anything from short-term Treasury bills or commercial paper to long term government or corporate bonds—had locked in when buying the securities and any change in yield as interest rates subsequently rose or fell.[17] These swaps, that is, were a kind of derivative contract based off of markets for a variety of interest-bearing assets, while the futures contract was a derivative of that derivative. DRW believed that the difference between short-term and longer-term interest rates would widen, and that when the effect of that worked its way through the swap market to the futures on swaps, it could unwind its position at a profit; most swap deals, however, took the oppositive view.[18]

DRW had an additional way it believed it could profit from trading IDEX U.S. Dollar Three-Month Interest Rate Futures contracts on the NASDAQ OMX Futures Exchange. This was because the International Derivatives Clearinghouse that handled the IDEX future paid cash, its "variation margin" when the daily settlement of the futures placed a higher value on trader's long positions. DRW's in-house analysts believed that the way the clearing house calculated this overstated the present value of a long position in the future in relation to the underlying swaps.[19] The clearing house calculated the variation margin, using a formula based primarily on bids and offers on each of the fourteen different IDEX futures contracts made between 2:45 p.m. and 3 p.m., and adjusted by the prevailing interest rates for over-the-counter swaps in trades the day before.

As Wilson and his in-house mathematicians analyzed the formula, they concluded that it would almost always produce a daily settlement that would generate a variation margin payment on long positions, in a way that the majority of traders at the time, playing the short side, did not seem to see.[20] It also meant that bidding in those critical 15 minutes between 2:45 p.m. and 3 p.m. could have a disproportionate impact— especially since canceling those bids before they could be hit meant DRW incurred no cost. Some of those bids were as much as 1.04 percentage points above the swap rate, the Commodity Futures Trading Commission found.[21]

The settlement period tended to be where all the trading action in the IDEX futures occurred. On February 25 2011, for instance, when the twenty-fourth trading day in a row, there had been no activity before the settlement period, DRW offered 250 futures in each of nine different maturities of the Three Month future (2,250 contracts in all), between 2:51 p.m. and 2:53 p.m. Minutes after the settlement period ended but when trading notionally continued, DRW cancelled those offers. When averaged in with any other bids, offers or completed transactions, the result was a settlement price six to seven percent higher than those on corresponding prices of over-the-counter swaps.[22] The Commodity Futures Trading Commission's investigation found that DRW had done pretty much the same on at least 118 days between late January 2011 and mid-August, when it closed out its long futures position, involving at least 1,032 bids in the ten- and thirty-year maturity that generated variation margin for the long position it had staked out in late 2010. The commission calculated that these bids generated some $20 million in unlawful profit for the firm.[23]

DRW's trading and its impact on settlement prices drew complaints almost from the start. In February, when an official from another firm trading the IDEX future called Wilson to complain about DRW's trading conduct, calling it unfair and manipulative, Wilson said DRW's bids "go up at 2:45 every day so they make sure the marks screw other people … You get to set the mark."[24] Jeffries and Co. initially seemed to shrug off DRW's trading—"You won big. We lost big," Jeffries chief executive officer Richard B. Handler wrote in an email to Wilson[25]—but later launched an arbitration complaint against the clearing house and the NASDAQ OMX Futures Exchange. Jefferies argued that the exchange and clearing house had mispresented the IDEX Three Month future as "economically equivalent" to an over the counter swap. The market, Jeffries argued, had failed in two of its primary functions: setting a real price for the variation payment it had to make and that DRW received and providing price discovery for an underlying asset; the swap in this case.[26] DRW's response was that there was a significant pricing differential between the future and the swaps, and backed up its case with a paper by one of its in-house analysts.[27] In dismissing any allegation that DRW had manipulated the market, the clearing house, as well as the arbitrator of Jeffries and Judge Sullivan in essence accepted Wilson's view that he knew the true value of the future because he and his analysts had understood it better than everyone else: the market worked here to produce a valid price. Despite this, the NASDAQ OMX exchange decided that December to drop the IDEX future. Though it did not say so, this decision suggested that the exchange agreed with Jeffries about the market was functionally disconnected from the swaps market where it was supposed to offer a way to hedge and a means of price discovery.

For the Commodity Futures Trading Commission, the issue was not market failure. The agency had faith that free markets would produce true prices, as long as nobody manipulated them. Encouraged by its successes with the DiPlacido and Amaranth "banging the close" cases, confirming as they did the Henner decision, the commission decided to pursue a case against Wilson and DRW. It argued that the floods of DRW bids that hit the market only during the settlement period amounted to a manipulation since they were so far off other prices, since there were so many and since DRW canceled them within minutes, before anyone could strike a deal. DRW just wanted to move the daily settlement price that would determine the daily variation payment it received (and that the shorts would have to pay to the clearing house so it could pay DRW).[28]

The commission argued that DRW knew there were no other participants in the market leaving it free to make uneconomic bids at inflated prices, that "day after day for seven months DRW's traders were shouting into an empty trading pit ...Their voices echo back to them because no one else is there."[29] Wilson himself testified that he directed DRW traders to bid for futures contracts for years where the firm did not have a position so that graph of settlement prices for the fourteen different IDEX futures "didn't have a bunch of weird kinks in it. So I was aware of all that and certainly involved in discussing with the traders how we were putting those prices in and moving them around."[30]

For Sullivan, the CFTC's argument that DRW was banging the close was just a slogan and the unfilled, quickly canceled bids were as legitimate a price as any completed transaction, since "sophisticated market participants would surely have accepted [DRW's] open bids if they thought they were above market value." Sullivan wrote.[31] Yet others in the market had in fact complained about DRW, rather than seeing its bids as proposing high prices that would have yielded a fast profit, as had been the case with Marlowe King's response to David Henner's limit-up 41.85 cent bid for the November shell egg futures price. DRW's higher than the market bids, expressed as interest rates, were at the same time lower-than-the-market bids for the underlying assets of the swaps that in turn were the underlying assets of the IDEX futures. Moreover, while DRW was bidding to buy a notional, future interest rate difference between daily changes in short term interest rates and the fixed rate coupons on long-term bonds, what it was doing was selling a contract, as was the case with Henner's 41.85 cent bid. The dynamic here was much like what Beccaria described when wheat farmer bringing twelve bags of wheat to the marketplace to freely complete with another farmer with just four bags for fifteen barrels of wine that vintners have on offer, the big farmer can move the price of wheat from the (roughly) one barrel of wine that would clear all the wheat and all the wine to a higher price of wheat in terms of wine.[32]

Beccaria's large wheat farmer could have proposed one counter argument—the question of who was buying and who was selling and how much wine and wheat changes hands—when Judge Sullivan wrote that "It is not illegal to be smarter than your counterparties in a swap transaction ...In the summer and fall of 2010, Don Wilson believed that he comprehended the true value of the Three-Month Contract better than anyone else ... and put his firm's money at risk to test it" [33] After all, since DRW canceled its bids, Wilson had not actually risked anything. In the end, Sullivan wrote "there was nothing wrong with [DRW] recognizing the flaw in the contract. ... and taking advantage of it," the judge he continued. "That's what markets are for."[34]

But that is not what markets are for.

Markets are for the exchange of goods and services. It is what happens, or does not, after an exchange that is when tests for flaws and fairness happen, whether that is in a settlement price formula in a contract so flawed that a commodity exchange drops its IDEX contract, or, as the landmark case establishing the *caveat emptor* (buyer beware) rule in the United States, a judge says tough luck to the buyer who thought he had purchased brazilleto wood (Haematoxylum brasiletto, or Mexican logwood, used for dye, medications and for string instrument bows) but ended up with "peachum" or trash lumber.[35] A market price might not, as Adam Smith suggested, always reflect the real value—what he called the natural price—since, as the examples Cesare Beccaria and Anne-Robert-Jacques Turgot proposed, it is not always the case that even the simplest models balance supply and demand. "Is there any evidence to indicate that [DRW traders] were making bids above, north of, their fair value point?" Judge Sullivan asked one Commodity Futures Trading Commission witness. "I haven't seen any evidence of what their fair value is at all," the commission witness replied.[36]

For Sullivan, this was one more piece of evidence that DRW's bids had not created an artificial price, and that therefore the firm had not manipulated the price of the future. While one possible reading of the commission witness's comment is what the NASDAQ OMX market concluded: that there really was no value to futures contracts on swaps, the same reading possible with the demise of the shell egg futures market in the 1970s, that is not really the point I want to make, tempting as it is. Instead, I will just say their remoteness from the commerce they purported to reflect—whether lending money or selling fresh eggs—offer an especially unobstructed view of the way that the very human dynamic of buyer and seller can generate an artificial price. Neither scale of trading nor sophistication of traders prevents unreal pricing, as we can see with the arbitrage trade in energy futures and swaps or U.S. Treasury bond futures and options on futures, or with the spoofing cases—flooding markets with quickly canceled bids or offers—in the extremely active futures markets in Treasury bonds, gold, silver, interest rate swaps, a stock market index, copper, gasoline, crude oil and light sweet oil.[37]

I would like to argue just for a moment that markets, in the abstract, idealized way Judge Sullivan and many economists use the term, are really metaphors for a difficult-to-predict and at times impossible to analyze interaction between two individuals. The question, then, is whether the best and most universally-applied metaphor is something like "The tumult; the color; the frenzy of activity; the people rushing about, shouting at the top of their voices and acting out their mysterious incantations," that Chicago Mercantile Exchange chairman Leo Melamed said drew him as a teenage message runner to the commodity futures business, giving him "an innate understanding of the laws of supply and demand" and "the beauty of the free market process."[38] I do not think it always is.

By narrowing our focus away from the exciting tumult of Melamed's trading floor to a David Henner or DiPlacido, microeconomics too can shift attention to the people who actually decide what the price of something will be. A more microscopic look can test the metaphor of battle that Herrell DeGraff used to equate shoppers in supermarket aisles pondering whether they can afford the price posted for ears of corn or packages of bacon or cartons of orange juice to trades of futures in corn or pork bellies or frozen concentrate orange juice serve, in theory, a price discovery role for the wider world of producers and consumers. In those supermarkets, and as it turns out, in most other transactions, the seller dictates a price and the buyer takes or leaves it—rather as what happened with DRW's bids for futures on swaps of interest rate income from differing debt securities. This microeconomic view of price, I think, may support a microhistory that suggests free markets can, at least sometimes, get prices wrong.

One indicator, in addition to the lack of bids and offers in supermarket aisles is to ask how often prices actually change—while remembering Paul Samuelson's view that the rapidly fluctuating prices of a futures market trading pit (or ever-shifting bond or share or swaps prices on modern trading rooms' computer screens) are simply the white noise that serves as a mathematical demonstration that prices are properly balancing demand and supply.[39] So, for example, Dennis Carlton found steel prices remained unchanged on average over nearly a year and a half of producers' sales to customers; chemicals for nineteen months, cement for seventeen months and petroleum products (in which there are active futures markets) for eight months.[40]

Alan Blinder, after surveying executives of mid-sized to large firms concluded that less than fifteen percent of goods and services produced in the United States were repriced more often than once a quarter, with fifty five percent repriced no more than once a year. The market signals from rises or falls in sales volumes only prompted price changes three to four months later, he found. Two of the most common reactions to market signals about changes in demand was to adjust auxiliary services, such as delivery timings and to hold off changing prices until seeing others move: both were cited by about two-thirds of executives as reasons why prices might not move. Nearly as many said the idea of an implicit contract with customers—that there were long term relationships they did not want to upset—as reasons to hold off changing prices.[41] Frederic Lee's review of some seventy-one studies of business pricing found that firms announce prices before starting to sell and since their efforts to sell unfold over time, business owners and managers find stable prices are efficient, in terms of managing costs, creating customer good will and avoiding price wars.[42]

Such administered prices are not market-clearing prices—that is, they do match supply to demand at any single point in time, and so not change as demand shifts and sales volume rises or falls—they do not move "in the virtually non-existent market or enterprises 'demand curve'," as he put it.[43] In essence, most prices are the result of business owners or managers' calculation of costs (generally speaking, average costs, however calculated) plus a mark-up, whether based on an internal target or conventional view about an appropriate return, which can (and usually does) vary from industry to industry.[44] In any event, a decision by a person or small panel of people who end up with something rather like Adam Smith's "higgling and bargaining of the market" that is "sufficient for carrying on the business of common life."[45]

Yet there have been times when the kind of markets I have been looking at in this microscopic way throw out prices that make the business of common life relatively difficult to carry out. There is, for example, the case of the artificial prices of natural gas or California electricity futures and swap contacts with cash flows pegged to future contracts' daily settlements fuel sudden spikes in electric bills—or, as happened in California, when those prices signal changes in the flow of electricity that a relatively fragile electric grid could not handle, forcing rolling blackouts.[46] Bubbles—persistently artificial prices, at least until they crash—can seem inherent features of financial markets, and the degree to which they rise to artificial levels and stay there seems to increase in proportion to the volume of purely speculative trades; trades, that it, to buy something that will soon be resold and not used or to sell something only fairly recently bought, and not made.[47] A stable equilibrium can emerge when students and other similar subjects playing in simulated, laboratory markets, though often this takes a few iterations and lessons learned, but this is not the case when such simulations deal in goods that can be traded again for a capital gain—shares of stock, futures in shell eggs, for instance.[48]

Experiments to simulate bubbles gave players cash to trade a financial asset that paid $0.24 at the end of each of 15 trading periods to the holder: its value should have started at $3.60 and declined by $0.24 at the end of each period, hit the bid/offer match typically started below $3.60 and then rose, hitting prices in later trading periods of as much as

$6, a value reflecting the ratio the players' cash to the amount of the asset available.[49] One model of financial market bubbles proposes that there are two types of actors: fundamental investors and "momentum" traders. The fundamental investors buy when they see securities (or derivatives) trading at a discount to a fundamental value and sell when they see those assets (or underlying assets) trading at a premium; the momentum traders react to rate of change in prices: but fundamental values in this case are what individuals perceive; momentum, matter of calculus.[50] Demand and supply schedules here, as CFTC Commissioner James Stone noted in the Indiana Farm Bureau case, are intangible, mere mental constructs.[51]

There are other mental constructs at play when people determine prices, and price, like those constructs, can be artificial. Karl Polanyi's "essence of bargaining behavior," the back and forth of higgling—even if, as in the shell egg futures pit, it is a single exchange: "41.85" and "Deal!" or "Yours!" or whatever Marlowe King called back—is what makes a market where "exchange at fluctuating prices" means "the element of antagonism ... is ineradicable."[52] It can be seen when John Hoekstra confronted David Henner, accusing him of unfair dealing, when the brokers and clerks from the clearing firm Lee B. Stern & Company dragged Darryl Zimmerman from the floor of the Chicago Board of Trade or when Amaranth Advisors trader Matthew Calhoun messaged his boss "Pain everywhere" as he executed Brian Hunter's scheme to force down the price of natural gas futures. The momentum trader's calculation of the rate of change of price suggests a focus on moment by moment fluctuation that is why a Dee Belveal would say Henner's 41.85 cent deal did not force a false price because "I can't conceive of manipulation being on a split-second basis."[53] Reflex can explain a lot about price in a financial market, just as much as mistaken perception and incomplete information might, even for those with faith in the efficiency of a free market, for, as Belveal himself would write, despite the hypothesis that a market price results from a balancing of supply and demand, it is what he called trading interests—buyers and sellers as well as those who are opting not to buy or sell—are the ones who create what he called the effective market price; something, that is, rather like Adam Smith's exchange price in contrast to his natural price. "Since reality never quite succeeds in attaining the 'perfect market's perfect dissemination of total information,' traders must always make their decisions from an uneven amalgam of hard facts and wispy conjecture."[54]

In the end, as the economist and successful futures market speculator John Maynard Keynes put it:

> Most, probably, of our decisions to do something positive, the full consequences of which will be drawn out over many days to come, can only be taken as a result of animal spirits – of a spontaneous urge to action rather than inaction, and not as the outcome of a weighted average of quantitative benefits multiplied by quantitative probabilities.[55]

Manipulation or animal spirits or reflex to match bid with offer of a resaleable financial instrument, the point is that, notwithstanding the theory, artificial prices can occur in a free competitive market. What had Henner done, then? Questioned by a Commodity Exchange Authority referee early in the case, asking "why did you wait until right at the bell and bid the limit up, rather than posting a bid earlier in the day at a substantially lower price?" Henner replied:

> "There weren't any more sellers at that point. Nobody wanted to sell the eggs."
> "Are you telling us, sir, that you knew that somebody would take a bid at a lower price all day long?" the referee asked.
> "No," said Henner. "We have a free market. There is no way of knowing what price people are willing to buy or sell."
> "Why didn't you put up a bid at a lower price, sir, is all I am asking?"
> "What would be the advantage of putting a bid up if nobody is willing to sell."
> "Did you know nobody was willing to sell?" the referee asked.
> "I don't trade that way."[56]

But the way Henner did trade, as his own witness, Dee Belveal, pointed out had in fact produced an artificial price, although he did not call it that. For "There is no profit to be made in posting a high price. ... You have simply made a bad buy and I submit to you that ... whoever put that high price on that trading range on the 25th of June, had to have made one of the worst buys in his life, because the next day the market was down a hundred - I don't know - a good long way. So he was wrong."

NOTES

1. "David G. Henner, retired trader, sailed the world," *Chicago Tribune*, June 24, 1994, 31.
2. Ted C. Fishman, "Busted," *Chicago Reader*, October 3, 1996, https://chicagoreader.com/news-politics/busted-6/. Barnaby J. Feder, "Clearing Firm's Worst Nightmare," *New York Times*, November 1, 1992. D-1; "Two Traders Indicted In Board of Trade Fraud," Ibid., July 22, 1993, D-2.
3. Fishman, "Busted". While Zimmerman here, like Henner with his egg futures and pork bellies trading, was outside the "core insider" network of rules-makers and customs-enforcers who Mark W. Geiger argues exert disproportionate influence in financial markets, he, like Henner, was able to force a price not by knowing anything special about the underlying assets of a derivative but by sensing the dynamic of momentary reactions in a competitive market. Mark W. Geiger, *Floor Rules: Insider Culture in Financial Markets* (New Haven: Yale University Press, 2024); Floor Rules: The Unwritten Code of the Exchange Mark W. Geiger Paper presented at the Society for the Advancement of Socio-Economics Annual Conference, July, 2014.
4. Complaint, In the Matter of Anthony J. DiPlacido et al., U.S. Commodity Futures Trading Commission Docket 01-23, 5.
5. Opinion and Order, In the Matter of Anthony J. DiPlacido, Commodity Futures Trading Commission Docket 01-23, Commodity Futures Law Reporter 30974-5.
6. Ibid., 30975.
7. Ibid., 30976.
8. Ibid., 30976–30977.
9. Ibid., 30977. Andrew N. Kleit, a professor of energy and environmental economics at Pennsylvania State University, after listening to tapes of Kristufek's call to DiPlacido, says Kristufek's "clearly agitated" tone and profanity point to an urgency that supports his testimony before CFTC that he was merely trying to unwind a hedge, rather than force a higher settlement price. Andrew N. Kleit, *Modern Energy Market Manipulation* (Somerville, Mass: Emerald Publishing, 2018), 66.
10. Opinion and Order, In the Matter of Anthony J. DiPlacido, Commodity Futures Trading Commission Docket 01-23,

Commodity Futures Law Reporter 30970, 30971, citing In re Henner, 1194.

11. DiPlacido v CFTC 364 F. App'x 657 (2nd U.S. Circuit Court of Appeals, 2009), 660.

12. Complaint U.S. Commodity Futures Trading Commission v Amaranth Advisers LLC et al. U.S. District Court, Southern District of New York, 07 CIV 6682, Exhibit A, 2–3, 4, 7. e.

13. Lawyers practicing before the commission were quick to see this, as with, e.g. Aitan D. Goelman, "Decision in DRW Makes It Even Harder For The CFTC To Prove Up Manipulation Compliance & Enforcement" (January 22, 2019) article posted by New York University Law School's Program on Corporate Compliance and Enforcement.   https://wp.nyu.edu/compliance_enforcement/ 2019/01/22/decision-in-drw-makes-it-even-harder-for-the-cftc-to-prove-up-manipulation/ and the briefing from the giant Clifford Chance business law firm "U.S. Court Affirms Economic Realism and Rejects CFTC Bid to Expand the Offence of Price Manipulation" (December 2018). https://www.cliffordchance. com/briefings/2018/12/u_s_court_affirmseconomicrealisman dreject.html.

14. Opinion, Commodity Futures Trading Commission v. Donald R. Wilson and DRW Investments, 13-civ-7884 (U.S. District Court, Southern District of New York, 2018), 8 (Sullivan was sitting by designation in the U.S. District Court for the Southern District of New York).

15. MF Global suffered major liquidity problems in 2011, and later that year would admit it had used nearly $900 million of customers' funds to mask shortfalls at its broker-dealer and British operations. When the company was unable repay those customers, it filed for protection from its creditors under the U.S. bankruptcy law, in theory to allow it to reorganize but it was instead almost immediately liquidated. MF Global Petition for bankruptcy, https://www.pacermonitor.com/view/4ZI XNXQ/MF_Global_Holdings__nysbke-11-15059__0001.0.pdf.

Kathleen Cronin, general counsel, CME Group, December 13 2011 letter to Rep. Randy Neuberger, chairman House Subcommittee on Oversight, "RE request for information regarding collapse of MF Global, https://financialservices.house.gov/upload edfiles/cme_group_response.pdf.

Azam Ahmed, Ben Protess and Susanne Craig, "A Romance With Risk That Brought On a Panic," New York Times, December 11 2011,D-1.

16. Opinion, CFTC v Wilson., 9.
17. Pricing a swap and determining which party pays and which is paid involves a formula in which a security that pays a floating rate (either because it is pegged to short-term interbank loan rates or because of changing secondary market prices for the security) is subtracted from the sum of the calculated value of present values of cash flows from the coupons on a fixed rate bond of the same maturity.
18. Complaint CFTC v Wilson, 14.
19. Opinion, CFTC v Wilson, 4, 5.
20. Ibid., 7, 11.
21. Ibid., 19.
22. Ibid., 20–21. For the IDEX three month, seven-year maturity DRW's bid of 3.174% was 17.9 basis points above the over the counter swap; for the eight-year, its bid of 3.403% was 20.7 basis points over; for the nine-year, its bid of 3.6% was 20.7 basis points over; for the 10-year, which was one of DRW's actual holdings of futures contracts, it bid 3.747%, or 20.8 basis points over; for the twelve-year, its bid of 3.976% was 20.7 basis points over; for the fifteen year, its bid of 4.201% was 20.8 basis points over; for the twenty-year, its bid of 4.473% was 30.8 basis points over; for the twenty-five-year, its bid of 4.554% was 30.6 basis points over and for the thirty year, the maturity in its actual long futures position for which it sought its variation margin, its bid of 4.597 was 30.7 basis points over. As Wilson said, DRW bid on all maturities so ensure that the settlement price curve they generated created the upward sloping line that mirrored (if it did not match) the yield curve for real interest-paying securities. Ibid.
23. Ibid., During the trial, evidence showed that DRW's settlement period bids during the period totaled 1,766, these bids, as on February 25 would have involved several maturities, so the number of futures DRW claimed it was willing to buy numbers in the hundreds of thousands; some 1,024 bids for the multiple maturities were used to determine the settlement prices for the relevant ten and thirty year maturities that generated the variation margin

payments to DRW. Memorandum and Opinion CFTC v Wilson, 11.

24. Ibid., 21.
25. Ibid., 13.
26. Ibid.
27. Opinion, CFTC v Wilson 10. This paper calculated "the difference between the [Three-Month Contract] and the corresponding uncleared swap rate [was] around 18 basis points for 10-year and about 60 basis points" for the 30-year maturity, Sullivan's opinion noted but without noting that these differentials far smaller than the differentials between DRW's bids and the market.
28. Complaint, CFTC v DRW, 12.
29. Opinion, CFTC v Wilson 23, quoting post-trial briefs and trial transcript.
30. Ibid., 19.
31. Ibid., 11.
32. Cesare Beccaria, *Elementi di economia pubblica* (Milan: G.G. Destafanis, 1804 [posthumous publication of lectures from1768-1770]), 348.
33. CFTC v Wilson, 26.
34. Ibid., 24.
35. Seixas and Seixas v Wood, 2 Cai R 48 (1804, New York Supreme Court of Judicature) at 55.
36. Opinion, CFTC v Wilson, 14.
37. Order, In the matter of J.P. Morgan Chase and Co, CFTC Docket 20-69; Order, In the Matter of the Bank of Nova Scotia, CFTC Docket 20-27; Order, In the matter of HSBC Bank, CFTC Docket 23-26; Order in the Matter of Belevedere Trading, CFTC Docket 19-45; In the matter of Simon Posen, CFTC Docket 17-20; In the matter of Sunoco LP, CFTC Docket 20-75; In the matter of Daniel Shak and SHK Management, CFTC Docket 14-03.
38. Leo Melamed, *Leo Melamed on The Markets: Twenty Years of Financial History as Seen by the Man Who Revolutionized the Markets* (John Wiley & Sons, 1992), 1, 219.
39. Paul Samuelson, "Proof That Properly Discounted Present Values of Assets Vibrate Randomly." *The Bell Journal of Economics and Management Science*, Vol. 4, No. 2 (Autumn 1973), 369; "Proof That Properly Anticipated Prices Fluctuate Randomly" *Industrial Management Review*, Vol. 6, No. 2, (Spring 1965), 41–49.

40. Dennis W. Carlton, "The Rigidity of Prices," *American Economics Review*, Vol 76, No. 4 (September 1986), 637–658.
41. Alan Blinder, "Why are Prices Sticky? Preliminary Results from an Interview Study," *American Economic Review*, Vol. 81, No. 2 (May1991), 89–96.
42. Frederic Lee, *Post Keynesian Price Theory* (Cambridge: Cambridge University Press, 1999), 212.
43. Ibid., 213, n 23.
44. See, e.g. Philip W.S. Andrews, *On Competition in Economic Theory* (London: Macmillan, 1964); A, Asimakopulos, *An Introduction to Economic Theory: Microeconomics* (Oxford: Oxford University Press, 1978); Alfred Eichner, *The Macrodynamics of Advanced Market Economies* (Armonk, NY: M.E. Sharpe, 1987); Michal Kalecki, "Costs and Prices," in M. Kalecki (ed.), *Selected Essays on the Dynamics of the Capitalist Economy* (Cambridge: Cambridge University Press, 1971), 43–62; Gardiner Means, "N.R.A., A.A.A. and the Making of Industrial Policy," in *Industrial Prices and Their Relative Inflexibility. Letter from the Secretary of Agriculture, Transmitting in Response to Senate Resolution no. 17, a Report Relating to the Subject of Industrial Prices and Their Relative Inflexibility* (Washington, U.S. Government Printing Office, 1935).
45. Adam Smith, *An Inquiry into the Wealth of Nations*, Book I, chapter v, paragraph 4.
46. David Ress, "Interruptions of Power: A Dark Side of Business," *The Star-Ledger* (Newark, N.J.) January 29, 2001, A1.
47. Sabiou Inoua and Vernon Smith "A Classical Model of Speculative Asset Price Dynamics," *Journal of Behavioral and Experimental Finance*, Vol. 37 (2023), https://doi.org/10.1016/j.jbef.2022.100780.
48. John Dickhaut, Shengle Lin, David Porter, and Vernon Smith, "Commodity Durability, Trader Specialization, and Market Performance," *Proceedings of the National Academy of Sciences*, Vol. 109 (2012), 1425–1430.
49. Vernon L. Smith, Gerry Suchanek and Arlington Williams, "Bubbles, Crashes, and Endogenous Expectations in Experimental Spot Asset Markets," *Econometrica* Vol. 56 (1988), 1119–1151; Gunduz Caginalp and Donald Balenovich "Asset Flow and

Momentum: Deterministic and Stochastic Equations." *Philosophical Transactions Royal Society of London*, Vol. 357 (1999), 2119–2133.

50. Momentum traders buy when dP/Pdt > 0 and sell when dP/Pdt < 0; Vernon L. Smith, "Causal Versus Consequential Motives in Mental Models of Agent Social and Economic Action: Experiments, and the Neoclassical Diversion in Economics," ESI Working Paper 18-11 (2018) Economic Science Institute. Retrieved from https://digitalcommons.chapman.edu/esi_working_papers/249.

51. In re Indiana Farm Bureau Cooperative Association and Louis M. Johnston, Docket 75-14, Opinion and Order, (Commodity Futures Trading Commission, 1982), 31, https://www.cftc.gov/sites/default/files/idc/groups/public/@lrceacases/documents/ceacases/indiana-johnston-dec1982-9.pdf.

52. Karl Polanyi, "Semantics of General Economic History" (New York: Columbia University Research Project on Origins of Economic Institutions, 1953), 12.

53. In re Henner, 1250.

54. Belveal, *Charting Commodity Market Price Behavior*, 233 (emphasis in the original).

55. John Maynard Keynes, *The General Theory of Employment, Interest and Money* (New York: Harcourt Brace & Co., 1936), 161.

56. In re Henner, 1183, 1185–1186.

References

Commodity Futures Trading Commission v. Donald R. Wilson and DRW Investments, 13-civ-7884 (U.S. District Court, Southern District of New York, 2018)

DiPlacido v CFTC 364 F. App'x 657 (2nd U.S. Circuit Court of Appeals, 2009)

In re David G Henner, 30 Agricultural Decisions 1151

In re Indiana Farm Bureau Cooperative Association and Louis M. Johnston, Docket 75-14, Opinion and Order (Commodity Futures Trading Commission, 1982)

In the Matter of the Bank of Nova Scotia, CFTC Docket 20-27

In the Matter of Belevedere Trading, CFTC Docket 19-45

In the Matter of Anthony J. DiPlacido et al., U.S. Commodity Futures Trading Commission Docket 01-23

In the matter of HSBC Bank, CFTC Docket 23-26

In the matter of J.P. Morgan Chase and Co, CFTC Docket 20-69

In the matter of Daniel Shak and SHK Management, CFTC Docket 14-03

In the matter of Simon Posen, CFTC Docket 17-20

In the matter of Sunoco LP, CFTC Docket 20-75

Seixas and Seixas v Wood, 2 Cai R 48(1804, New York Supreme Court of Judicature)

U.S. Commodity Futures Trading Commission v Amaranth Advisers LLC et al. U.S. District Court, Southern District of New York, 07 CIV 6682

Ahmed, Azam, Ben Protess and Susanne Craig: "A Romance With Risk That Brought On a Panic," *New York Times*, December 11, 2011, D-1

Andrews, Philip: *On Competition in Economic Theory* (London: Macmillan, 1964)

Asimakopulos, A.: *An Introduction to Economic Theory: Microeconomics* (Oxford: Oxford University Press, 1978)

Blinder, Alan: "Why are Prices Sticky? Preliminary Results from an Interview Study," *American Economic Review*, Vol. 81, No. 2 (May1991), 89–96

Caginalpm Gunduz and Donald Balenovich: "Asset Flow and Momentum: Deterministic and Stochastic Equations," *Philosophical Transactions Royal Society of London*, Vol. 357 (1999), 2119–2133

Carlton, Dennis: "The Rigidity of Prices," *American Economics Review*, Vol 76, No. 4 (September 1986), 637–658

Clifford Chance: "U.S. Court Affirms Economic Realism and Rejects CFTC Bid to Expand the Offence of Price Manipulation" (December 2018) Note to Clients

Dickhaut, John, Shengle Lin, David Porter, and Vernon Smith, "Commodity Durability, Trader Specialization, and Market Performance," *Proceedings of the National Academy of Sciences*, Vol. 109 (2012), 1425–1430

Eichner, Alfred: *The Macrodynamics of Advanced Market Economies* (Armonk, NY: M.E. Sharpe, 1987)

Fishman, Ted: "Busted," *Chicago Reader*, October 3, 1996

Goelman, Aitan "Decision in DRW Makes It Even Harder For The CFTC To Prove Up Manipulation Compliance & Enforcement" (January 22, 2019) New York University Law School's Program on Corporate Compliance and Enforcement.

Inoua, Sabiou and Vernon Smith "A Classical Model of Speculative Asset Price Dynamics," *Journal of Behavioral and Experimental Finance*, Vol. 37 (2023), https://doi.org/10.1016/j.jbef.2022.100780

Kalecki, Michal: "Costs and Prices," in M. Kalecki (ed.), *Selected Essays on the Dynamics of the Capitalist Economy* (Cambridge: Cambridge University Press, 1971), 43–62

Kleit, Andrew: *Modern Energy Market Manipulation* (Somerville, Mass: Emerald Publishing, 2018)

Lee, Frederic: *Post Keynesian Price Theory* (Cambridge: Cambridge University Press, 1999)

Means, Gardiner: "N.R.A., A.A.A. and the Making of Industrial Policy," in *Industrial Prices and Their Relative Inflexibility. Letter from the Secretary of Agriculture, Transmitting in Response to Senate Resolution no. 17, a Report Relating to the Subject of Industrial Prices and Their Relative Inflexibility* (Washington, U.S. Government Printing Office, 1935), 1–3

Polanyi, Karl: "Semantics of General Economic History." (New York: Columbia University Research Project on Origins of Economic Institutions, 1953)

Ress, David: "Interruptions of Power: A Dark Side of Business," *The Star-Ledger* (Newark, N.J.) January 29 2001, A1

Smith, Adam: *An Inquiry into the Wealth of Nations*

Smith, Vernon L.: "Causal Versus Consequential Motives in Mental Models of Agent Social and Economic Action: Experiments, and the Neoclassical Diversion in Economics," ESI Working Paper 18-11 (2018) Economic Science Institute

Smith, Vernon L., Gerry Suchanek and Arlington Williams, "Bubbles, Crashes, and Endogenous Expectations in Experimental Spot Asset Markets," *Econometrica* Vol. 56 (1988), 1119–1151

INDEX

The manufacturer's authorised representative in the EU is Springer
Nature Customer Service Centre GmbH, Europaplatz 3, 69115 Heidelberg,
Germany. If you have any concerns regarding our products, please
contact ProductSafety@springernature.com

Printed and bound by CPI Group (UK) Ltd, Croydon, CR0 4YY

28/04/2026

02098473-0005